SAINT
IN THE
WILDERNESS

The Story of Isaac Jogues,
Missionary and Martyr in the New World

SAINT
IN THE
WILDERNESS

The Story of Isaac Jogues,
Missionary and Martyr in the New World

GLENN D. KITTLER

DOVER PUBLICATIONS, INC.
Mineola, New York

Bibliographical Note

This Dover edition, first published in 2013, is an unabridged republication of
the work originally published by Doubleday & Company, Inc., Garden City,
N.Y., in 1964 under the title and subtitle *Saint in the Wilderness: The Story of St.
Isaac Jogues and the Jesuit Adventure in the New World.*

Library of Congress Cataloging-in-Publication Data

Kittler, Glenn D.
    Saint in the wilderness : the story of Isaac Jogues, missionary and martyr in
the New World / Glenn D. Kittler.
        p. cm.
    Summary: "The New World was a dangerous and mysterious wilderness
when Isaac Jogues and his fellow missionaries arrived in 1636 to convert the
Native Americans to Christianity. Written in simple but stirring terms, this
true story of the intrepid Jesuit's adventures and hardships among the
Algonquins, Hurons, and Mohawks is as thrilling as any fiction"— Provided
by publisher.
    Reprint of: Saint in the wilderness. — Garden City, N.Y. : Doubleday, 1964.
    ISBN-13: 978-0-486-45718-5 (pbk.)
    ISBN-10: 0-486-45718-4
    1. Jogues, Isaac, Saint, 1607–1646. 2. Jesuits—Canada—Biography.
3. Missionaries—Canada—Biography. 4. Christian saints—Canada—
Biography. I. Title.

BX4700.J564K5 2013
272'.9092—dc23
[B]

                                                            2012041451

Manufactured in the United States by Courier Corporation
45718401
www.doverpublications.com

To John J. Delaney

CHAPTER ONE

THE WONDERFUL news had been completely unexpected and made the young man happier than he had ever been. Four Jesuit seminarians at the College of Clermont, in the heart of Paris, were to be ordained ahead of schedule and sent immediately to the missions in New France, and he was one of them. The news was wonderful in many ways. Its evidence of the urgent need for more priests in New France was proof of the success of the Jesuit missions there. The mere fact that the missions were flourishing was also proof of the effective and peaceful French rule in the new colony. But to Isaac Jogues, the best part of the news was that it would make him a priest and a missionary more than a year sooner than he had hoped.

It was January, 1636, and Paris was under a blanket of snow which had fallen before Christmas and lingered. Ordinarily, the Jesuit ordinations would have been held in June and families of the ordinands would have traveled from the ends of the earth, if necessary, to witness the great event. But now the roads were bad and travel difficult. And there was no time. Waiting in French ports were ships ready to dash across the Atlantic at the first hint of spring. The ships would not wait for their families. Thus at the end of January the four seminarians—Isaac Jogues, Charles Garnier, Pierre Chastellain, Paul Ragueneau—were ordained in the college chapel in the presence of the Jesuit community.

[7]

There had been a period recently when Isaac Jogues doubted that he would ever reach the priesthood. He had always been a brilliant student, but then he encountered the subtleties of theology and they staggered him. His studies came hard. For a while, he seriously considered putting them aside and becoming a Jesuit lay brother. Only by the sternest application was he able to labor his way through the complex subject, and he was still looking forward with dread to another arduous year of it when the news came that he was soon to be ordained, that his studies had come to an end.

He wrote his mother immediately, telling her first of the special blessing which he considered the news to be and then expressing his regret that, because of the circumstances, she would be unable to witness the ordination which meant almost as much to her as it did to him. He added that, in view of the urgency, he probably would not have the opportunity to return to his home parish in Orleans to celebrate his first Solemn High Mass.

Madame Jogues would not hear of it. She knew, however, that it was useless to insist that he ask his superiors for permission to come home. Just the year before he had refused to request a similar permission in order to attend his sister's wedding. At first, Madame Jogues suspected that the Jesuit superiors, as an exercise in holy obedience, had refused the permission, but Isaac assured her in a letter: "It never entered my mind to speak of the matter to my superiors. The urgent duties of my work do not permit me to leave the house even for a single day. Moreover, my presence at this ceremony was not at all necessary. The prayers that I am able to offer for the happy result of this marriage are as helpful from afar as they would be near."

But a first Mass was something else. This time, Madame Jogues decided not to leave the decision to her son. Instead, she wrote his superiors, suggesting that since she had given her favorite son to the Jesuits for life would it not be a simple kindness on their part to return him for a few days so that she could have the joy of beholding him at the altar just once before they shipped him off to the other side of the world. The Jesuits bowed. Early in February, Isaac Jogues found himself in a coach, careening southward over the muddy, gutted roads on the seventy-five mile trip to Orleans.

The Jogues of Orleans were a prominent and affluent family, deriving their income from business enterprises in the city and sizable estates in the country. Isaac Jogues's father, Laurent, like all heads of the family, held public office. Laurent Jogues's first wife, a member of minor royalty, died after presenting him with two daughters; his second wife, Françoise, whose family was also successful in business, gave him six sons and a daughter. Isaac, born at two o'clock on the morning of January 10, 1607, was the third son. And he became his mother's pet. He took after her side of the family; fair, slender, rather delicate in appearance and shorter than others his age, flashing dark eyes, well-bred by nature as well as by circumstances. He received his early education at home from his mother and private tutors; at ten he entered a Jesuit school attended by sons of only the best families. At seventeen, he announced that he wanted to become a priest.

His mother was pleased. As a Catholic mother, Madame Jogues was aware of the special honor it was to have a son called to the priesthood. In this case, there was a particular reason for happiness. As a priest, Isaac would never be separated from her as completely as her other sons, who had married and had become preoccupied with their own families. He would always be available to provide her with love, attention and comfort. A widow now, she needed this. Furthermore, with the boy's intelligence and the family's position, there was every likelihood that he would go far in the

Church: he might even become a bishop. It seemed proper that a Jogues should expect to reach such heights.

All these expectations fell apart when Isaac explained that the kind of priest he wanted to become was a Jesuit priest. This changed the picture entirely. It meant, among other things, that he would have to go wherever the Jesuits sent him, and Madame Jogues would have nothing to say about it. Jesuits worked as teachers and missionaries all over the world: her "dear Isaac," as she always called him, might be assigned to some horrible place and forced to live in the worst circumstances. The prospect saddened her and she tried to dissuade him, but he was adamant and he got his way.

For the next twelve years, Madame Jogues saw little of her son, scarcely more than a week or two a year, and sometimes not even that. She suffered because Jesuit rules prevented her from swamping Isaac with daily shipments of the delicacies he had enjoyed at home. Only the happiness that glowed in his letters comforted her to the point of resignation where she could admit that he had made the right decision. His letters came regularly—from Rouen, where he spent two years in the novitiate; from La Flèche, where he studied philosophy for three years; from Rouen again for four years, where he taught in a Jesuit college; and then from Clermont in Paris, as he struggled with theology. Then came the letter with the news of his ordination and his imminent departure for New France, the letter promptly followed by one from Madame Jogues to the Jesuit superiors —and he was on his way home.

He had changed. Years of prayer and study had made him quiet and reflective. Still in the first glow of ordination, he was preoccupied with gratitude to God for the gift of holy orders. He had always been a warm and outgoing person, and he continued to be, but now there was a certain reserve about him, acquired through a solemn realization of both the responsibilities and opportunities endowed him by his priesthood. He was now a man of God in a particular way, equipped with faculties which could send a soul to Heaven. For this reason he cherished his priesthood and he was determined to keep it unblemished. He was God's, and he lived now only to make all others His.

His mother noticed the change. Father Isaac's first Mass was scheduled for February 10, the first Sunday of Lent. He reached home early in the week, at the height of the pre-Lenten carnival. Orleans was one big party. Because of the special reason for joy in the Jogues household, there was even greater festivity. The young priest was the center of it. Relatives, friends, neighbors all packed the house, eager to congratulate Isaac, to drink to his long life. He accepted the attention with amiable restraint, appearing in the main parlor whenever a new crowd arrived, acknowledging the congratulations with a smile and polite gratitude, giving his blessing when it was requested, then unobtrusively withdrawing to his own room when the visitors turned to wine and food, holiday gaiety and local gossip. Only his mother witnessed his subtle escapes, watching him depart with a gaze that was long and sad.

On the eve of Ash Wednesday, Isaac drew his mother aside and said: "I want to spend the next four days in retreat, preparing for the Mass. I have arranged for a room at the Jesuit college in town. I'd rather not see anyone, if you don't mind."

She had expected something like this. "As you wish, my dear," she said, studying him seriously. Then: "Isaac, are you very happy?"

He brightened. "Oh, yes, Mother. I couldn't explain how happy."

"You seem so withdrawn."

He shrugged. "My priesthood was a sudden thing. I guess I'm not used to it yet."

She put a hand to his shoulder; he leaned forward and they touched cheeks. "My pet," she said, "and I hardly know you. I wish you weren't going away." His quiet smile told her this was a wish he could not grant. "I shall miss you painfully."

"We'll be together at the altar every morning," he assured her.

"Yes." But she could not bring herself to be satisfied with that. How old was he now? Twenty-nine. She had sent a boy to the seminary and a man had come home: she had missed out on the best years of his life. She could not even call him her own any more: he belonged more to the Jesuits than to her. She tried to console herself by thinking of the countless mothers who had suffered this precise aching sense of loss since the day when the Blessed Virgin watched her Son, almost the same age as Isaac, leave the house at Nazareth to begin His priesthood and never to return. How had Mary been comforted? Surely God must somehow fill the gap; she hoped so.

She put on the smile she often used to erase unpleasant thoughts. "You have not minded all the people?"

"Not at all."

"Everybody wanted to see you."

"I enjoyed seeing them."

She patted his hand. "Very well, my dear, off to the college with you. I'll have the carriage brought around. Is there anything you need? Anything that I can do?"

"You have already done too much."

The four days were richly rewarding. In his prayers and meditations, Isaac concentrated on the nature of his priesthood, still as pure and fresh upon him as spring dew. The retreat provided additional spiritual stamina for him to become the kind of priest that both God and his vows required, strong in virtues, in the world but not of it, ready for any trial. On Sunday, he donned the purple vestments of Lent and followed the procession into the college church, crowded with the people who had called on him at home early in the week. His mind was only on the Mass, the magnificent prayer of it, the holy sacrifice of it. At the consecration, when he bowed at the altar to breathe the words by which he would transform bread and wine into the Body and Blood of Jesus Christ, there were tears in his eyes. Minutes later, he turned and faced the congregation, the sacred species held in his right fingers, the ciborium in his left hand, and he waited until his mother alone knelt at the Communion rail to be the first to receive the Lord from him.

CHAPTER TWO

1

EARLY MONDAY morning, Isaac took the coach for Paris, content that his farewell with his mother had not been as wrenching as he had feared. She, too, seemed to have changed. At the party after the Mass, she had been proud and beaming. There had been a family discussion of a gift for Isaac. He insisted he needed nothing: the Jesuits would take care of him from now on. But Madame Jogues was adamant, her old directorial self. She bought him the chalice and vestments he would use at Mass in the New France missions. They fitted neatly into a small black satchel that was destined to become as much a part of his daily life as his breviary.

At the good-by, Madame Jogues had knelt for Isaac's blessing; then, rising, she took both his hands in hers and drew him to her, and as he kissed her cheek she whispered: "Write me!" They separated a moment, then he embraced her briefly before climbing quickly into the coach. She put on her familiar, practiced smile, now a defense against tears, and there was just time for her to raise her hand to wave as the coach pulled away. In the coach, Isaac tightly gripped the handle of the small black satchel.

Back in his room at Clermont College, Isaac was amazed by the assortment of books and papers he had collected during his three years as a theology student. The papers were meaningless to anyone but himself and he discarded them easily, but the books were something else. How he had struggled through them! Now they were like old enemies who, the war over, had suddenly become close friends. Isaac felt downhearted as he surrendered the books to the college librarian to be turned over to the younger students coming along. The books had opened new worlds for Isaac; now he was about to go out into the world for which they had prepared him.

On Wednesday, accompanied by the three young priests who had been ordained with him, Isaac Jogues left Paris for the Jesuit house at Rouen and his thirty-day retreat. At the end of March, spiritually refreshed and strengthened by their month of prayer and meditation, the four new missionaries arrived at the seaport of Dieppe, eager to be on their way to their new lives in the New World.

It was a new world indeed, and in the minds of many European adventurers it was still little more than a pathway to the riches of the Orient. France, England, Spain and Holland had established colonies on the Atlantic shores of the vast and mysterious continent, but still they looked westward for a short route from Europe to the East. One hundred and seventeen years after Christopher Columbus had discovered the New World, Samuel de Champlain, the French explorer, reached Lake Huron and confidently believed that the treasures of Cathay were just beyond.

It was John Cabot, an Italian navigator sailing in 1497 under the British flag, who was the first European to set foot in what became known as New France. He thought he had reached India and that the strangely dressed people who approached him were Indians. Because they did not understand Cabot when he asked where he was, the "Indians" answered with their own word for welcome: "Kanata." Cabot believed they had said "Canada," and when he returned to England he announced that he had reached Canada, presumably somewhere on the northeast coast of India. On his second trip, Cabot hoped to bring back some of the gold and gems of India, but bad weather swept his fleet northward and he managed to obtain only a few furs from isolated Indian hunters he encountered at Labrador. This discouraged his backers, and Cabot died before he could convince them to let him try again.

In 1534, on August 10, the feast of St. Lawrence, a French expedition under Jacques Cartier sailed into a great bay on the Canadian coast, and Cartier named it after the saint. The swift current moving across the bay indicated to Cartier that an enormous river must empty into it: he located the river and gave it, too, the name of St. Lawrence. Over a hundred miles upstream, Cartier came upon a gigantic bluff that soared three hundred feet into the air. An astonished crewman exclaimed, "Que bec!"—which in his Norman dialect meant "What a rock!" Cartier climbed the bluff, planted the Cross and the French flag at the top of it, and proclaimed that the magnificent domain spread before him now belonged to France.

The following century was darkened by European wars, and thus it was not until 1608, seventy-two years after Cartier had climbed the Quebec bluff, that Samuel de Champlain established the first white settlement in New France, on the site of Cartier's camp at the foot of the bluff.

Circumstances were developing which would affect Canada's future for another hundred years. First, Catholic France was itself torn internally by the religious wars; even the royal family was split. King Henry III, a Catholic, had died in 1589, and the throne went to his sister, Marguerite, then married to Henry of Navarre. Because French law prohibited rule by a woman, the throne automatically went to her husband, who became King Henry IV. But Henry IV had been raised a Protestant. He had led Protestant armies against Catholic armies; he had even fought against his father-in-law at one point, then on his side at another. Leading Catholics of France did not want to accept Henry as their king, with the result that he had to fight five more years before Paris—and the throne—fell to him. During these years he became a Catholic, reportedly saying, "Paris is worth a Mass." While he was entering the city, a student tried to kill him, and when the King learned that the student had been attending a Jesuit college he accused the Jesuits of breeding insurrectionists; he closed the college and banned the Jesuits from France.

At this time, the Society of Jesus—the Jesuits—had been in existence about fifty years and had already given the Church saints, great educators and courageous missionaries. The Society had grown rapidly in number and influence: in this short time, it had over a thousand members and had served the popes on important missions throughout Europe. Because of the Jesuit special pledge of service to the popes, it was inevitable that when, from time to time, a king found himself at odds with a pope the Jesuits found themselves in the middle. Moreover, the French Protestants loathed the Jesuits because of their aggressive identity with the Church, and it was suspected that one motive behind King Henry's stern action against the Society was more to appease his Protestant friends than to avenge the attempt on his life.

Further evidence of appeasement appeared in 1603, when the King awarded a charter to exploit the natural resources of Canada to the Company of Merchants, a group of businessmen most of whom were Calvinists. A Catholic exception in the Company was its chief geographer, Samuel de Champlain, a devout man who had fought with the Holy League in the religious wars. His earlier expedition to the West Indies best qualified him to lead the Canadian exploration; in 1603 and 1604 he surveyed the Atlantic Coast as far south as Cape Cod, and the St. Lawrence River as far inland as the mountain-capped island Cartier had named Mont Réal. On his third trip to New France, in 1608, he traveled up the river of the Iroquois and discovered the lake which still bears his name. It was on this journey that an event occurred which profoundly affected the future of France in the New World.

There were two areas of conflict brewing in the territories of the New World then being settled, one new and one old, each different yet both alike, and both destined to become related. The new conflict was the imported feuds of Europe, with the French along the St. Lawrence, the Dutch on the Hudson and the British in Virginia. Although the Dutch and British had fought France in the religious wars, they themselves were not allies except in one effort: as France, united and strengthened under Henry IV, increased its activity in the New World, both the Dutch and British were determined to prevent the French expansion at any cost and by any means.

The second conflict also involved three nations, Indian nations—the Algonquins along the St. Lawrence and the New England coast, the Iroquois stretched across what became New York State, and the Hurons on the shores of the lake named after them. The Iroquois were by far the most powerful. Unlike the Europeans, there were no alliances of any kind among the three Indian nations: their three-way war had gone on for years, and even within each nation were clans with old grudges which often sent them into battle against each other.

The two conflicts became related as the European settlements increased. The French discovered they could trade and live peacefully among the Algonquins on the St. Lawrence, and the Dutch discovered the same with the Iroquois in New York. It was, however, an uncertain peace, for the settlers never knew when the unpredictable Indians would turn on them. As long as the Europeans had the advantage of possessing muskets, there was the hope that the Indians would think seriously before attacking only with their arrows. But then the fatal mistake was made.

In 1609, Champlain decided to go west to make contact with the Hurons and enter into a peace pact with them. His small force of French troops was accompanied by a band of Algonquins, both for protection and to lead the way through the wilderness. At Ticonderoga, they came upon an Iroquois war party. Fighting broke out, which ordinarily the Iroquois would have won, but the presence of the French brought muskets into the battle and the Iroquois suffered a rare and serious defeat. Champlain went on to the Hurons, leaving behind in the defeated Iroquois a deep and abiding hatred for the French. No Frenchman, they vowed, would ever again walk away from them alive. The Dutch now had an unexpected and powerful ally in their own opposition to French expansion in the New World, and they took advantage of the situation by equipping the Iroquois with muskets in the process of their subsequent tradings. In years to come, these muskets would be used when the Iroquois joined the British against the French both in Canada and the American Midwest.

Meanwhile, King Henry IV, eager to consolidate all France behind him, moved to assuage his Catholic critics by lifting the ban on the Jesuits, not only allowing them back into the country but also awarding them grants to reopen their old schools and build new ones. Champlain sent word to the King that he felt the time had come to send Catholic missionaries to evangelize the Indians. The Calvinists at Quebec strongly objected to the idea, but when they realized that they were going to be overruled they relented, insisting, however, that the missionaries should not be Jesuits. As a gesture of compromise, the King chose four Franciscan Recollet Fathers. It was hoped that, over the years, the Recollets would add to their number, but they were unable to do so because of a shortage of vocations.

Then King Henry died, his throne passing to his wife, Queen Marie, as regent for her young son, Louis XIII. The Queen was a close friend of Cardinal Richelieu, now rising in influence. When, in 1625, the Recollets asked that the Jesuits be sent to their aid, Richelieu approved the request despite opposition from the Protestants. Upon arriving in New France, the five Jesuit missionaries were forbidden by the Calvinists to land at Quebec, and it was therefore necessary to go three miles farther up the St. Lawrence to an abandoned fort Cartier had built. To the Jesuits, this was immaterial. Their joy was in being in New France, in being able to work with the Indians at last, in being able to demonstrate once again the Jesuit skill in the missionary effort.

Meanwhile, the British were beginning to realize their mistake in not giving John Cabot additional support in his explorations in Canada. By now it was too late for the British to make any priority claims on the country. But this was the period of the Thirty Years' War, in which the French were deeply engaged, so the British resorted to other tactics. British vessels threatened French settlements along the Canadian coast. In 1628 three French Protestants, backed by British interests, led an expedition up the St. Lawrence for an attack on Quebec. The town held out for several months, until food and ammunition were gone. One of the first acts of the victorious British force was to round up the five Jesuits, ship them first to Virginia, then back to France, and with that it seemed that the Catholic influence in Canada had been put to an end.

So it might have been, but for Cardinal Richelieu. He was now the most influential man in France. Enraged by the loss of Canada, Richelieu notified the British that he would not accept the fall of Quebec as the final curtain on French authority in the colony. The British, ready to fight the

French on the far side of the Atlantic, were unwilling to risk a war at home, so they suggested negotiations. For three years the negotiations dragged on inconclusively. Finally, in 1632, Richelieu sent word to London that he would give the British thirty days to produce an acceptable compromise or he would order the French fleet to Quebec to exterminate the British holdings there. The ultimatum carried the threat of a war of total involvement, and it was effective: the British withdrew from Canada entirely.

The land grants which King Henry had awarded his Calvinist friends in the Company of Merchants were still in effect. Regarding the French return to Canada as an opportunity for a clean sweep, Richelieu dissolved this group and replaced it with the Company of the One Hundred Associates, a group of Catholic investors, to whom he turned over the development of New France with the understanding that they would support both colonization and the missionary effort among the Indians. Richelieu favored the Capuchins, but when he offered them the assignment they said they were not equipped for such an enormous undertaking. The Cardinal then turned to the Jesuits.

Within a few weeks the first band of Jesuit missionaries was on its way across the Atlantic. Now, four years later, as the stormy weeks of March, 1636, drew to a close, Isaac Jogues waited at Dieppe to make the same journey.

Years before, when Jogues had first applied for admission into the Jesuit seminary, he was asked why he wanted to join the Society. "I want to go to Ethiopia," he said, "to be a missionary there and to die there."

The seminary dean studied the young man for a few silent moments, then said: "No. You will die in New France."

It was a prophecy, and now the stage was set for it.

Crossings usually took over two months. For this reason, ships that left France too late in the spring were forced to spend the year in Canadian ports rather than risk a winter return on the storm-rent North Atlantic. The eight ships at Dieppe had been scheduled to depart on March 16, but lingering storms held them back. For just such an event, the Jesuits kept a house at Dieppe where the departing missionaries could spend their time as they awaited the call to board their vessels. Isaac Jogues knew it would be months, perhaps a year, before his letters from New France reached home, so he used his waiting days to write his mother, supplying her with enough to read and reread during the long silence ahead. He was excited, very happy, and his letters showed it. He gave his mother details of Dieppe, of his ship, which he had visited, of the men with him, he repeatedly assured her of his love and gratitude and prayers, and realistically he wrote: "May God reunite us in His holy Paradise if we do not see each other here on earth."

On the morning of April 8, the skies cleared. The word went out: today. Isaac hastily finished his latest letter home, then hurried to the wharf where small boats waited to take the Jesuits to their ships at anchor in the bay. In order that each crew might have the benefit of a priest, the Jesuits had been assigned to various ships. The Jesuits also had their mission appointments. Isaac Jogues was assigned to the Huron villages on a great lake about a thousand miles west of Quebec. His ship, however, was going only as far as the village of St. Charles on the island of St. Louis de Miscou in the Baye des Chaleurs in the Gulf of St. Lawrence, and it was his responsibility to make his way to the

Hurons as best he could. He did not worry: he would reach the Hurons if he had to walk.

Sharp winds, the aftermath of the storms, caught the eight ships a few hours out of Dieppe and sent them briskly across the sea. With such winds, it was possible to make up for lost time, and now there was every likelihood that the eight ships could visit their various ports, discharge supplies and take on cargoes of fur, wood and fish, and still have time to rendezvous and make the journey back to France before the winter set in.

At the end of May, only seven weeks after leaving France, the hills of Newfoundland were low on the starboard horizon. The ships passed through Cabot Straits into the great gulf; then, one by one, they turned off to head for their assigned ports of call. It was on the morning of June 2 that Father Jogues's ship entered the calm Baye des Chaleurs and dropped anchor off St. Louis de Miscou Island. There were three or four small fishing craft in the bay. From the shore came a swarm of canoes. Ashore, Isaac could see a cluster of log cabins; atop one of them was a cross. The uncertain circumstances of mission life made it impossible for the Jesuit leaders in Paris to know where a particular missionary might be at any particular moment, and so Jogues had no idea which of his confreres would be awaiting him on the island when he arrived. For that matter, because of the suddenness of his appointment to the missions, the young priest was not expected. So there would be surprise on both sides.

There was no wharf. As the ship dropped anchor in the bay, canoes, manned by Frenchmen and Algonquins, began to streak out from shore. Father Jogues, the lone passenger to disembark at Miscou, waited impatiently at the ship's railing for a canoe to come alongside. At last one arrived, bearing two Frenchmen. Isaac said quick good-bys to the ship's captain and others nearby; then he went over the side on a rope ladder. Below, the two settlers steadied the canoe by bracing themselves stiff-armed against the ship as the priest descended.

"Watch your step, Father," one settler said as Jogues lowered one foot into the canoe.

His first impulse was to shake hands with his welcomers, but the second man said: "You'd better sit, Father. These things overturn easily."

He sat. "I'm Isaac Jogues," he said, eager to establish an identity in this new place.

"Welcome, Father. Two of your confreres are here at Miscou."

"Yes? Who?"

"Father Du Marché and Father Turgis."

"How wonderful." He had known them both at Clermont; they had been ordained the year before. He smiled as he envisioned their own surprise at seeing him a year ahead of time. His satchel and suitcase were being lowered on ropes and he reached for them, dangerously rocking the canoe.

"Try not to move, Father," one settler said. "I'll get them."

Embarrassed by his awkwardness in the fragile craft, Jogues settled carefully. In a moment, the two Frenchmen began to paddle toward shore. Nearby, other canoes, manned mostly by Indians, hovered gingerly in the white caps of the bay, awaiting cargo. The Indians were short and heavy-set, with long, wiry hair, their copper-colored naked bodies painted blue and red with dyes made from flowers and roots, and they called to each other in guttural barks which were unintelligible to the new missionary but sounded glorious to him because of their assurance that he was at last among the people he would help bring to God.

He looked ahead. In the small crowd on the beach he could see Du Marché and Turgis, their hands cupping

their eyes for a better view in the bright sun. One of them—
was it Turgis?—pointed, and the two priests moved near
the water. Soon the mild surf lifted the canoe and sent it
smoothly into shallow water; the two Frenchmen stepped
quickly out of the craft and guided it onto the sands to a
hissing stop. Isaac scurried out and ran to his friends, and
immediately the three young Jesuits were a maze of em-
braces, a cacophony of greetings. In a noisy cluster, they
made their way up the beach to the cabin with the cross,
and in the chapel they knelt to give thanks for Isaac's safe
trip; then they went into the primitive living quarters at
the other end of the cabin. They sat there talking far into
the night.

Nothing in even the best seminary training could prepare
a young missionary for the emotions which struck when
he finally felt under his feet the soil of his new home.
Although the Jesuit missionaries annually sent to France
detailed reports on their experiences in Canada, and Isaac
Jogues had read them, the experience of having actually
arrived himself must have been dazzling for him. As a
student, he had heard the tales of the Jesuits who had
been expelled from Canada by the British in 1628, but even
they could not adequately express the full sense of purpose
which arose in a man who realized that he was at last
where God meant him to be, about to embark on the work
God meant him to do. The happiness resulting from these
convictions produced an air of achievement, of maturity,
even in a newcomer, and Jogues, like men before him and
men after him, surely experienced the gratifying sensation
of suddenly becoming useful to God, like being born full
grown.

Du Marché and Turgis—both named Charles—had been
deposited at Miscou Island by the French fleet which had
left Dieppe in the summer of 1635, and they had spent
the winter on the island. Some twenty Frenchmen were

[25]

living there, engaged in hunting, fishing, logging, trading; no one was certain of the number of Indians—perhaps a hundred or so—but they came and went too frequently for one to be sure how many called the island their home. As Algonquins, their homes could be anywhere along the northern shores of the St. Lawrence, westward to Quebec and beyond.

"Have you converted any of them?" Jogues asked, and his training had prepared him for a negative answer.

Turgis took the question with a shrug and a slow shake of his head. "It is not that easy. Their own ways are too deep in them."

"We baptize the dying, of course," Du Marché said. "But with the rest it is mostly a matter of getting to understand them, and vice versa. They are teaching us their language, and we use the lessons to ask them about their religion and tell them about ours. It is a slow method, but you cannot go too fast with these people. You will find that out for yourself when you are here awhile."

"I am going to the Hurons," Jogues pointed out.

"Yes, you mentioned that," Du Marché remembered. "When I saw a priest in the canoe I thought you were my replacement."

"Replacement?"

"A message arrived from Father Le Jeune. He wants me to go to him at Quebec. I was just waiting for your ship, in case there was anything on it I could take inland with me."

"You can take me," Jogues said quickly. The others grinned, enjoying the enthusiasm of the newcomer, which they had experienced themselves and never quite lost.

CHAPTER THREE

1

ISAAC JOGUES remained at Miscou for two weeks. Before his
ship reloaded and moved on down the coast to its other
ports of call, he wrote his mother and sent the letter off with
his ship, unsure when both would reach France. "I feel I
have entered Paradise," he wrote, but the observation was
based more on the fact that he was where he so much
wanted to be than on what he saw around him. The Miscou
settlement was small and poor; the people had worked hard,
with slim results; the winter had been severe, worse than
anything the French had experienced before, and although
the Indians were peaceful they were also unreliable, their
moods varying so much from day to day that the settlers
never knew where they stood. If there was peace at Miscou
it was because there was peace at Quebec, the area of the
major Algonquin clans. In winter when food was scarce, the
French fed the Algonquins from their own stores, and when
there was sickness the French doctors treated the Algonquins, undoubtedly saving many lives. Thus the word had
gone out from Algonquin leaders at Quebec that the French
were friends and should be treated that way throughout
the nation. But it was an uncertain alliance, depending
dangerously on the whims of the Indians, and no one could
be sure what those whims might be. On lonely Miscou
Island, isolated at the mouth of the bay, a change in the
wind was enough to turn the Indians sullen and send the

settlers to their cabins for their muskets. The men least disturbed by the Indian vacillations were the missionaries. The settlers had come to New France to make a better life for themselves; the missionaries had come to make a better life for the Indians. A century of mission effort had taught the Jesuits that usually some of their members had to die in the process of planting the Faith in a new land. So be it. An ancient Christian adage put it that in the blood of martyrs were the seeds of the Church. Very well. The price was high but the prize was worth it.

Charles Du Marché arranged with the owner of a fishing boat to take him and Isaac Jogues to Quebec. They left on the morning of June 13. In two weeks, Isaac had learned a great deal about life in New France, including the proper way to ride in a canoe. On the beach, he took off his shoes, not merely to keep them dry but primarily to avoid shoving a heavy foot clear through the thin birch hull. And he had learned how to relax, squatting and unmoving, his knees under his chin, for hours on end. This, he had discovered, was a torment only for the first five minutes, by which time he was too numb to feel any discomfort until the horrible moment when he had to face the torture of getting out and straightening up. This morning, however, he had only a five-minute ride ahead of him, out to the waiting, low-riding fishing boat. There he had the occasion to demonstrate another lesson well learned by swinging himself aboard the boat while scarcely rocking the canoe at all. He had quickly become a seasoned veteran.

Enormous, that was the only word for New France. Everything he saw made everything back in France seem like a miniature painted with an eyelash—the trees, the animals, the birds, the fish, the rivers. Isaac was sailing up the St. Lawrence for two days before he realized he was actually between its banks, seventy miles apart.

He shook his head. "How long is the river?" he asked Du Marché.

"Who knows?"

"How far west does New France extend?"

"Who knows that?" They both shook their heads.

After ten days, they reached a point where the river was narrow enough to see both banks. This was Tadoussac, where the larger ocean-going vessels anchored for the winter or waited impatiently in high summer for their cargo to come down-river on smaller boats. Three of the ships that had crossed with the fleet that had brought over the new Jesuit missionaries were already there, eager to get away. Jogues learned that some of his confreres had already gone on to Quebec; he looked forward to joining them.

On the morning of July 2, Isaac Jogues and Charles Du Marché got their first glimpse of the great rock at Quebec—another New World enormousness to stagger them. The Jesuits had two houses at Quebec, one in the town atop the bluff, where Father Paul Le Jeune, Superior of the mission, kept his office, and the other in the abandoned fort they had inherited from Cartier. Landing, Jogues and Du Marché made for the fort, which they knew to be the headquarters for transients, and their arrival exploded more of the familiar wildly joyful greetings. It was strange and wonderful, this reunion with dear friends here on the majestic threshold of a new world and a new life. There was something of a homecoming in it, warm, boisterous, instantly knowing, and yet it was distinctly more exciting because of the great unknowns that awaited all of them.

Eight missionaries were at the fort when Jogues and Du Marché arrived, some of them their former professors, others veterans of the first Jesuit attempt in New France now sent back because of their valuable experience, and there was Paul Ragueneau who had been ordained with Isaac. Two faces were missing, the other former ordinands.

Isaac asked: "Where are Charles Garnier and Pierre Chastellain?"

"On their way," said Ragueneau, his voice thick with envy. "Off to the Hurons."

Jogues was dismayed and disappointed. "But I was to go with them."

Father Le Jeune said, "We did not know when you would get here. Besides, it was a surprise even for Charles and Pierre. The Hurons will be arriving at Three Rivers in a few days to do their summer trading, and they sent word ahead that they wanted two priests to take back to their villages with them. It was the first time they have asked, an important sign of progress. We dared not hesitate, for fear they'd change their minds."

Isaac understood. "And when do I go to them?"

Le Jeune shrugged. He sensed the young priest's disappointment, but there was nothing that could be done. "We'll see. Soon, I hope."

At least he was in Quebec. The fort stood where the Lairet Stream emptied into the St. Charles River, about a mile from where the St. Charles emptied into the St. Lawrence. It was surrounded by a fir palisade, each pole at least fourteen feet high, each wall about a hundred feet long. There were two buildings, one a workshop, the other the priests' living quarters, part of which also served as their chapel. The sleeping accommodations were six small cubicles, but now there were ten priests at the mission, which meant they had either to take turns sleeping on the floor or make the hike each night to the rectory up in the town. Outside the stockade were vegetable gardens and pastures for the cattle.

Isaac Jogues was given free rein. Because of the uncertainty of his immediate future, it was suggested by Father Le Jeune that Jogues not attempt to learn the local Indian dialect: should he be assigned a hundred miles away the dialect would be almost useless. "Just wander around and get used to the place," Father Le Jeune had suggested, but Isaac felt uneasy with nothing to do. So, mornings, he went to the clinic in the workshop and helped dispense minor medications; then he would go to the vegetable gardens to help there in any way he could. In the afternoons, when he was not needed at the fort, he might go up to the town to visit the settlers and encourage them, to hear confessions, perhaps to baptize a baby. And there were, of course, his spiritual exercises—his Mass, his rosary, his meditation, his breviary, all of which combined to occupy him three or four hours a day. There was a new feature about his breviary. At home, priests were always seen with their breviaries in their hands wherever they went so that they could read the prayers of praise of God at the specified times each day. But in the missions a priest's hands were usually busy all the time, so the breviary was worn on a chain around the neck, immediately available to be read when designated or when possible. Newcomers like Jogues had difficulty at first getting used to the weight around their necks and the sharp slaps of the book against their chests when they walked too quickly; but the morning a fortnight later when Isaac Jogues skittered down the steep path to the river to say good-by to Father Le Jeune, he was already so accustomed to the innovation that he was scarcely aware of the book that beat against his chest with each jarring step. Father Le Jeune was going to Three Rivers. The Huron flotilla was expected there any day, and since Huron chiefs would be accompanying the traders it was fitting that the chief Jesuit of New France should be there to greet them.

"I wish I were going with you," Isaac said.

"Oh, you'll be heading out soon enough," Le Jeune consoled.

Isaac was on his way in a week.

[31]

The summons was unexpected and urgent. Apparently the Hurons had undergone a change of heart. Ordinarily they did not welcome strangers, especially white men, into their country, but already Garnier and Chastellain were traveling west on Huron invitation, and there was a feeling at Three Rivers that even more priests might be requested. In that event, Le Jeune sent word to Isaac Jogues to hurry to Three Rivers to be ready to accompany the Hurons back to their villages.

Actually, Three Rivers was a misnomer. There was only one river, the St. Maurice, but two large islands in its mouth gave Jacques Cartier the impression that three rivers were emptying into the St. Lawrence. By the time the mistake was discovered the name was set. Three Rivers had been an Indian trading center for years. When France regained Canada in 1632, settlers built a village in the hills of the larger island in order to take part in the trade. However, Jesuits had been at Three Rivers, even beyond, much earlier. The first mission, arriving in New France in 1625, had sent priests to make a study of conditions at Three Rivers, and one of them, Jean de Brébeuf, had spent two years out in the Huron country before the British victory which brought about the exile of the French. Now, as Jogues approached Three Rivers, de Brébeuf was back with the Hurons, impatient for more priests to help with the great task.

The canoe trip from Quebec to Three Rivers took two full days; Isaac arrived late at night. As his canoe entered shallow water, he hoisted himself deftly over the side, then reached for his Mass kit and small suitcase and walked ashore. On the beach, he dried his bare feet, then put on his socks and shoes. On the trip he had worn his soutane tucked into its sash, both for comfort and to keep it dry. Now he let his robe drop full length, and he hurried up the hill to the Jesuit cabin.

"Don't let your hopes get too high," Le Jeune warned when they were settled over a cup of tea. "You have an assignment to the Hurons, but you go only if they will accept you. With Garnier and Chastellain, we have five priests there now, plus four laymen, the most we have ever had. We need more, of course, but this depends entirely upon the Hurons. So far this year they have been very receptive. We can hope, but let's not hope too much."

"Very well," Isaac agreed, "I won't hope too much but I'll certainly pray all I can. Have the Hurons arrived?"

"Not yet. We have a letter," he held up the paper, "from Garnier and Chastellain, on their way out with the Huron advance party. The main Huron flotilla is being held up in the Ottawa River by the Island Algonquins. There may be fighting, unless the Hurons agree to pay the tribute the Island Algonquins want for letting them pass through. Garnier says the tribute is exorbitant this year."

"But I thought both the Hurons and the Algonquins were friendly to the French," Isaac said.

"They are," said Le Jeune, "but not to each other."

This was one of the puzzles of Indian relations. The Hurons and the Algonquins were distantly related; there was a similarity in their languages, but the Hurons had formed a confederacy with other tribes which, like them, lived in the interior along the northern shores of the Great Lakes. The Algonquins had stayed out of the confederacy, and this put them at odds with their cousins. For that matter, the Algonquins were at odds among themselves. The clans that lived along the St. Lawrence had adjusted to the French settlers and lived peacefully with them, but the clans along the Ottawa, particularly those who lived on the river islands, remained hostile. Like all Algonquins, those at Three Rivers had no affection for the Hurons but tolerated their presence during their annual trading visit because of the prosperity it meant for them. The Island Algonquins, however, lived too far from Three Rivers to profit from the trading, and so they offered the Hurons a choice of paying a tribute or fighting their way down the Ottawa.

The name of the Huron tribe was a misnomer, again due to the French. Most Huron men shaved their heads in a way that left a two-inch-wide furrow of thick black hair that ran from their foreheads to their napes, at which point the longer hairs were braided. The distinctive furrow reminded the Frenchmen of the brushy hair on the heads of French boars, called *les hures,* and from this Huron was easily derived. The Hurons were actually Wendat (or Wyandot) people, as were the other tribes in their confederacy. The confederacy had been formed as a defense against an even greater confederacy, the Iroquois Nation, which existed along the southern shores of the Great Lakes and the St. Lawrence, in what became New York State, and was composed of the Senecas, Cayugas, Oneidas, Onondagas and the Mohawks. The Iroquois were a savage, brutal, warring people, feared and hated by their neighbors to the north.

Isaac Jogues had the occasion to witness an example of that hatred the day after he arrived at Three Rivers. He was in the Jesuit cabin with Le Jeune when their conversation was interrupted by the distant sound of singing.

"Hurons?" Jogues asked eagerly.

Le Jeune frowned. "No. Algonquins. Hurry." And he rushed out the door.

Isaac rushed after him. "What's the matter?"

"It's a victory chant," said Le Jeune. "There must have been a fight. They have prisoners."

[34]

They reached the beach. It was crowded with Algonquin women, ripping off their clothes. As the approaching canoes rounded the final bend in the river and came into sight, a great cheer went up from the beach. The women plunged into the water and began to swim out to the canoes.

Le Jeune pointed. "Isaac, look. Those raised poles in each canoe. Tied to the tops—scalps. Must be twenty or thirty of them. Dear God!"

The swimming women had reached the canoes and clung to them, shouting. Isaac asked: "What do they want?"

"The scalps. They're supposed to be good luck. A woman who gets one believes that all her babies will be boys who will grow up to be strong braves. Look, there. Iroquois."

They were in the third canoe, a man and a woman, smaller, stockier, swarthier than the Algonquins, their black hair thick and straight. Their faces were stern and determined, and they, too, were singing, a fierce chant of defiance and revenge. The canoes slid into the beach.

Le Jeune said: "We must stop this." He ran into the crowd and tried to fight his way to the prisoners, but the Algonquins brushed him aside.

The Iroquois stepped ashore and the Algonquins flew at them, tearing off their clothes, beating them with fists, with stones and whips and thorny branches. It was the man they were mostly after, for he was the warrior, he was the threat and the danger. They leaped on him, biting his face, his shoulders, his arms and legs, drinking the blood they drew. And the man did not utter a sound.

Le Jeune was in the thick of it, struggling to pull the Algonquins aside. Isaac was too dazed to move. Horror filled his throat with vomit, his eyes with tears. Suddenly, enraged, he threw himself upon the savage maze and, like Le Jeune, fought to pull the Algonquins away. He could hear Le Jeune shouting in Algonquin, his tone a blend of pleas and anger.

Algonquin boys came running up the beach carrying burning branches. They made their way into the crowd and buried the flames into the Iroquois' body. The air filled with the stench of burnt meat. A woman cut off the man's thumb and tried to shove it into his mouth, but he spat it out. She laughed and picked up the thumb and took a flaming faggot from one of the boys and held the thumb to it until it was cooked, and she gave it to a child to eat.

The crazed mob moved upshore, dragging the prisoners and the priests. Le Jeune and Jogues still struggled to end the fury, and one here, one there, the people they pushed back remained aside, surprised by the priests' audacity. Gradually the panic subsided and there was only Le Jeune's voice, loud, angry, threatening. The people withdrew a little. Isaac went to Le Jeune's side. An Algonquin chief was standing near and Le Jeune barked the ugly language at him, pointing to the prisoners and then to the people.

The chief said something; the people turned and went away. A few braves surrounded the two Iroquois and led them off to a tepee, where a guard was placed around it. Then the chief walked away. Le Jeune and Isaac were left alone on the beach.

Their chests were heaving, their breath exploding from them, and wrenched nerves kept their arms twitching. Isaac put a hand to his face to wipe away tears that would not stop. "Is it over?" he asked.

"Yes."

"Oh, my God."

"Terrible."

"If I had not seen this with——"

"I have seen worse."

"Dear God." Isaac looked toward the prison tent. "What about them?"

"The man will die. The woman will become a slave."

"Terrible."

"Isaac, in the cabin is some holy water. Fetch it." Isaac looked around, hesitant, and Le Jeune said: "It is all right; it is all over. You are safe."

Jogues hurried up the hill to the cabin, found the holy water and took it to the prison tent and gave it to Le Jeune. The Iroquois lay on the ground. Chunks of him were missing; blood spurted from the wounds with each fading heartbeat. Le Jeune began the prayers of baptism as he administered the sacrament.

The woman was on the far side of the tent, squatting on her haunches, her eyes blank, unseeing. Her man died, but she gave no notice of it.

When the two priests left the tent and paused outside it, from down the beach came the sounds of the Algonquins, innocent, carefree, childishly lighthearted.

Isaac said: "They have forgotten it already."

"Yes. That is their way."

"What did you tell them that made them stop?"

"I told them that when winter comes and they are hungry and they have no food I will not give them any," said Le Jeune. "I told them that when they are sick I will not treat them, that when the Iroquois come to seek revenge, I will take their side. I told them I will not love them any more."

"And that was enough?"

Le Jeune sighed. "I don't know how distressed they were by the chance of losing my love. But the winters here are severe: there is never enough food and always much illness. In the past, the people simply suffered and died, but we have been taking care of them, sharing our supplies with them and treating the sick, and the recent winters have not been so bad. They remembered."

Jogues was impressed. "It's amazing that these people can experience gratitude."

"Oh, no," Le Jeune said quickly and sadly, "not gratitude, not that. Fear. They remembered in fear. You see, Isaac,

[37]

hunger and sickness are things these people cannot understand. It's impossible to convince them to plant bigger crops in the spring so they can have bigger harvests, a surplus to store up for winter. Each year they plant what they planted the year before. Winter comes, their food runs out, and they can't understand why this should happen to them. They usually suspect they are being punished by evil spirits for some wrongdoing, although there is very little they consider wrong. So if there is no other village nearby that they can raid, they either resort to cannibalism among their own or they just sit back and starve."

"Appalling."

"It is the same with sickness," Le Jeune went on. "If a man falls and breaks an arm or if he is wounded in combat, he is not too bewildered because he can see the cause and effect, though usually he will blame an evil spirit for it. But sickness, this invisible enemy who attacks silently each winter, is something else. The people cannot see it coming, they cannot fight it off, as they might an enemy tribe, and they cannot run away from it. Again they blame spirits, but they realize this is useless. So they watch each other die. Well, we have changed all that, at least a great deal of it. We have plenty of food. We have our cattle, and we get our shipments of prunes and figs and flour from France. We have our muskets, which are much better for hunting than bows and arrows, despite the experts these people are with them. So we can keep them from starving. And we have our medicines, limited though they are, and we can keep most of the people from dying of sickness. They know this now. They stopped torturing those Iroquois, when I reminded them of these things, not out of gratitude but out of fear that they would be cut off from the food and medicine, that their old unseen enemies would be free again to strike back at them. That is the way they are, Isaac. That is the mentality we are dealing with."

[38]

They began to walk up the hill to their cabin. They did not speak for a while, then Le Jeune said: "You won't forget what you saw here today."

"Never."

"You may see worse."

"No, please God."

"Don't let it embitter you. You will grow to love these people, Isaac. You must love them." Le Jeune's tone was almost pleading. He stopped and turned. "Look at them down there. You would not think that a few moments ago they were as they were. If you tried to tell them, they would deny it. They are like children most times, unable to see behind or ahead, only the now; and yet, like children, if we treat them as children they resent it. We have a great task, Isaac, and we will fail at it unless we resort constantly to the special strength we have: love."

They stood there, watching. Below them, the women were starting to prepare the evening meal. In the river were a few boys, splashing about. A canoe came around the bend: fishermen returning from their traps. Dogs, back from an afternoon of chasing squirrels and chipmunks, trotted out of the hills and sniffed around for their masters. The men were quiet, squatting in front of their tepees or in them, waiting for their meal. Down the beach, alone, stood the medicine man facing west, and he began the chant to the setting sun.

3

Days passed, and still there was no sign of the Hurons. The French settlers agreed that the Island Algonquins must be particularly obdurate this year. Of greatest concern were the ships waiting at Tadoussac for their cargoes to take back to France before winter fell. The ships could not return empty, and yet if the cargo was much later they would not be able to return until the following spring. The settlers at Three Rivers kept a worried eye on the river.

Then, one August morning, an unfamiliar canoe rounded the bend to the west. The French settlers on the hillside saw it first and they called the Jesuits for a look at it. Was it Huron? It seemed to be. But why just one canoe? Where were all the rest?

Down at the river Algonquins were already lining the shore, watching the Huron canoe nose in. The two Hurons in it stepped lightly to the beach, went directly to Father Le Jeune and handed him a letter.

"It's from Father Daniel," Le Jeune said, a little surprised. "He is traveling with them." He read on, then nodded. "Yes, they are late because of the tribute. The Islanders are willing to let Father Daniel pass through, but he feels he should stay with the Hurons in case there is any fighting. He doesn't think there will be: the Hurons are afraid they will get here too late to sell their furs and they are more willing to negotiate than they were earlier. It may be a few more days."

It was over a week. At last it swung into sight, the great Huron fleet, scores of canoes filling the broad river, hundreds of braves singing loudly and rhythmically beating their paddles against their craft between strokes. It was a magnificent sight. In one of the leading canoes was Antoine Daniel, singing, paddling, beating, and when he saw the Jesuits on the shore he waved happily.

Le Jeune said to Isaac: "I wasn't expecting him. You know what this means, don't you?"

"There will be a place for me when they go back?"

"Perhaps."

Now the Hurons were pulling their canoes up on the beach. Algonquins hurried about, helping. This was as far east as the Hurons would go: now it was up to the French to transship the pelts and furs on to Quebec and Tadoussac, a task which provided employment for the Algonquins and thus meant an income for them.

Antoine Daniel came ashore. The sight of him stunned his confreres. Isaac had seen him last in 1632 at Rouen, when they said good-by as Daniel left for New France; Le Jeune had seen him last that same year when they said good-by at Three Rivers when Daniel left for the Huron country. Now he was almost unrecognizable. He had lost a lot of weight, he seemed shriveled, he was a weary, worn, over-worked old man. He had spent four years with the Hurons at the village of Ihonatiria, on what became known as Georgian Bay, and the four years showed on him clearly, shock-ingly. One glance was all Le Jeune needed to see why Fa-ther Jean de Brébeuf, Superior at Ihonatiria, had sent Daniel back, and the same glance told him that Daniel's mission days were over. Daniel knew this too, and despite his efforts at gaiety he was saddened. Isaac Jogues was silent. In Daniel he saw himself in years to come. He was not dis-couraged or frightened; he was merely sobered by this liv-ing evidence of the trials that awaited him.

That night, the Hurons and the French held a council, exchanging presents, praise and pledges of friendship. Deal-ings with the Hurons required a good deal of tact. Like all Indians, they were suspicious of change and strangers: even between their own villages there was a deep wariness; and so, in order to placate the Hurons, the French found it nec-essary to refer repeatedly to their love for them. The French had certain plans for their new colony but they had learned from experience that it was useless and dangerous to come right out with them, for the Indians looked upon direct suggestions as orders, and they did not like orders. It was thus out of love, the French said, that there were certain things they wanted to do for the Hurons, and there were certain things that the Hurons, out of love, might be willing to do for them. The Huron view of love was uniquely

Indian: as long as the love was pleasurable, profitable and peaceful, he was willing to go along with it, but the moment it required sacrifice, selflessness or surrender he would have no part of it. He would kill his mother, his wife, his children, his best friend in a moment should they seem to endanger his own welfare, and he knew they would do the same to him. He felt the same way about the French.

The French had three ideas. First, they believed that the Jesuits, through religion, could provide a civilizing influence upon the Indians, so they wanted the Hurons to accept as many of the missionaries as possible. Second, the French felt there would be an advantage in the exchange of children—raising Huron children in French homes at Three Rivers or Quebec and letting French children be raised in Huron villages. The French children involved were orphans, brought over by the Company of the Hundred Associates. Experience showed that adult settlers often tired of the rigorous demands of colonial life and eventually wanted to go home. For the orphans, on the other hand, home was wherever they were put, and they were more apt to stay where they were put. Orphans raised by the Hurons would, the French thought, remain French at heart and, learning Huron ways and languages, would produce important links with the tribe, whereas the Huron children, raised in French atmospheres, would become more French than Huron and would be good allies when they finally went home. Out of the Jesuit influence and the children exchange there would result, the French hoped thirdly, an easier traffic of French interests in the Huron country, without the present expensive necessity of an army to protect the French explorers from sudden attacks. At the council, the French considered it prudent to touch only on the first two ideas.

The Hurons had misgivings. For the practical reasons of winter food and medical care, they were willing to accept a few Blackrobes, which they called the Jesuits because of their black soutanes, just as they had called the Recollets the Brownrobes because of their brown habits, but they did not want to be overrun with them. After all, the Blackrobes were useful just a few months of the year. What good were they the rest of the time? There had been few converts of good health; practically all baptisms had taken place at death moments, and some Hurons suspected the deaths actually resulted from the baptisms. Why invite more of the same uncertainty? As for the children exchange, the Hurons saw in it the subsequent loss of young braves to fight enemies, and this kept them cool toward the idea.

To proceed, therefore, required tact. "Sometimes," said the French spokesman at the council, "we feel that you do not love us as much as we love you. Is it not true that your lives are better since we are here? Do we not give you wampum for your furs, do we not give you tools to build better houses, do we not give you traps to hunt easier? Is this not proof of our love? And where is proof of your love for us? You will not exchange children; you refuse to see that these children will grow up to be true brothers and good friends, in good times and bad; by keeping the children apart you keep our peoples apart. And the Blackrobes. Only in one village do they find love, only in Ihonatiria are they welcomed, only at Ihonatiria do they live with their Huron brothers. What about you chiefs from other villages? If you permit the Blackrobes to visit you at all, it is only in winter when times are bad and you let them stay only a short while. Your coldness pains our hearts. We wonder if we have done right in choosing the Hurons to love."

The silent Hurons squirmed under such a weight of love. Really, had they been that bad? All along, they believed that the French were profiting equally as well in the trading: that sort of thing was to be expected or surely the trading would have ceased. Might it cease now? The Hurons hoped not. To be sure, they had profited thus far, but what they really wanted were muskets, which the French as yet had not been willing to give them. The Iroquois were getting muskets from the English and Dutch, and the Iroquois were an enemy of the Hurons, just as the English and Dutch were enemies of the French. Very well. Let there be an exchange of children this year: it would provide a basis for bargaining for muskets next year. But the Hurons would not mention this now. They would wait until the morning council when, by custom, it was their turn to speak.

The reference to Ihonatiria had offended a chief from Ossossané, a village on the same Lake Huron peninsula with Ihonatiria, and there was an old rivalry between the two. He sought out Father Daniel and sullenly asked: "Why did that man say what he did about my village?"

"What did he say?" asked Daniel.

"He said that Ihonatiria is a better village than Ossossané."

"Did he say that?"

"It sounded so to me. A man should not say things about a place he has never seen."

"I'm sure he did not mean it that way," Daniel consoled.

"I know how he meant it," said the chief. "He thinks there is more love for the Blackrobes at Ihonatiria because they are permitted to live there."

Daniel shrugged. "You can only measure a man's love by the way he treats you."

"Did I not always treat you well when you came to Ossossané?"

Daniel remembered his many visits to Ossossané when he had not been offered so much as a crumb. "Yes, you did," he said. "I used to think how pleasant it would be to live there all the time."

"Why didn't you ask?"

"As your visitor," Daniel pointed out, "it would have been improper of me to ask."

"Then I ask it," said the chief. "I ask it now."

Daniel smiled with true warmth. "You are very generous, my brother, but I don't think I will be returning to your country." He waited hopefully.

The chief frowned a little, then looked around. "What about the other Blackrobes here? Cannot one of them come to Ossossané?"

It had worked. "I will talk to my chief about it," Daniel promised. "Because it is you who makes the invitation, I am sure he will arrange it." The chief nodded, content, and walked away. Daniel went over to where Le Jeune and Jogues were talking. He said: "Isaac, I think your time has come."

CHAPTER FOUR

1

THE TRADING went on for four days. Isaac Jogues used the time preparing for his journey. He had little to pack: a few winter clothes, some trinkets to give to the Hurons as gifts, his Mass kit. Most of his preparation was spiritual. He was about to enter a world where there was no concept of morality as he understood it. He would see things and hear things from which his life as a seminarian for the past dozen years had protected him. Now he was a priest but he was still a man, and among the Hurons he would need special spiritual stamina if he was to remain a good priest. So he made a short retreat, begging God to strengthen him with patience and charity for the trials ahead.

He had a new name. When Father Le Jeune had introduced him to the Ossossané chief he had said: "This is Isaac Jogues."

"Ondessonk?" asked the chief.

"Isaac Jogues," Le Jeune corrected.

"Ondessonk," the chief said again.

Le Jeune said to Isaac: "Well, I guess Ondessonk it is. He can't pronounce your name, but he has given you an apt Huron substitute. Ondessonk. It means bird of prey."

"It is apt, isn't it?" said Isaac. "I intend to do a lot of preying upon the Hurons—for their souls."

"Good hunting."

Le Jeune advised Jogues on the conduct that would be expected of him on the trip. Although he had been invited to go to the Huron country, he was not to travel as if he were a guest or even a passenger. He was to work. He would not be expected to help paddle the canoe in which he rode, but he would have to help tote supplies over the many portages along the way, and he was to make himself useful at the morning and evening meal chores. He was to mind his own business but he must be friendly, cheerful and cooperative at all times. The impression he made on the Hurons during the trip would be the one they would report to their villages when they got home. His entire future with the Hurons, then, depended on his first few days with them.

Traveling with him would be a French orphan, Jean Amyot, ten years old, the first of the French children to be exchanged. The Hurons agreed to leave behind three of their boys at Quebec.

On the morning of Saturday, August 23, the Hurons began to pack their canoes. These chores, as such, did not concern Father Jogues, but he decided to take part in them in order to show the Hurons his willingness to work. He carried bundles down to the beach, then carefully observed the Huron method of packing them so that, in the future, he could pack them himself. Some of the canoes needed repairs: Jogues went into the woods to cut saplings which could be used as frames. At his side throughout the day was young Jean Amyot, who had also been told that the Hurons would expect him to work. The busy day passed quickly for both of them.

The next dawn, Father Isaac said his Mass, ate a breakfast of bread and coffee, aware that it would be the last such breakfast for a long time, then collected his effects and went down to the river where most of the settlement had already gathered to watch the departure. The air was crisp with tension. Ahead, everybody knew, lurked many dangers—the Iroquois who prowled along the southern banks of the St. Lawrence and the Island Algonquins in the Ottawa would be constant threats. And there were the dangers of the trip itself; the swift rivers, the rapids and waterfalls, the packs of wolves and foxes, the rattlers, the wildcats. Frenchmen who had traveled west with Champlain were acquainted with the many perils; merely watching others prepare for the same journey was enough to renew their fears.

The Jesuits, understandably, were primarily concerned about Isaac Jogues and the boy. The arduous trip would be most demanding upon them, and the Hurons would have no patience with them if exhaustion forced them to lag behind. Moreover, if anything went wrong—if there was a bad storm or an accident or an attack—it would not be unlikely for the superstitious Hurons to blame them for it and punish them, even kill them. Equally disturbing was the fact that even if everything went well and the expedition arrived safely in the Huron country, the Jesuits at Three Rivers would have to wait a year, until the next trading fleet came, to be sure.

The Huron leaders gave the signal and all the braves moved to their canoes. Jogues turned to his confreres for a final good-by and blessing, then led Jean Amyot to the water's edge. The two canoes to which they had been assigned waited in the shallows a few feet from the shore. Isaac lifted his soutane and tucked the skirt into the sash, then removed his shoes, waded out to his canoe and stepped expertly into it. As he settled in the required squatting position, he observed that young Jean was also safely aboard his craft.

They began to move out. From the shore came cries of farewells. Looking back, Jogues saw that Father Le Jeune was trying to shout a message to him and pointing repeatedly to his head. Then he remembered: he removed his broad-rimmed hat which, he had been told, blocked the

[48]

view of paddlers and was sometimes blown away and had to be retrieved, thereby irritating the Indians. He put on a stocking cap.

The braves swung their paddles with steady, deep strokes and the canoes cut into the broad river with smooth speed. A mile ahead was the advance party, watching for trouble from the shores. Scarcely a sound rose from the great flotilla itself. The four kneeling braves in Jogues's fifteen-foot canoe paddled on and on, without pausing, without speaking. He glanced over at Jean and saw the enchantment on the boy's face as his eyes examined the strange shores. An hour later, when he looked for Jean again, the boy was asleep. Isaac dared not sleep: he might stir, he might overturn the canoe. Besides, if he fell asleep the braves would suspect he had no endurance.

By mid-afternoon, the priest was uncomfortably hungry, but he had been forewarned that on the trip he could expect only two meals a day, at morning and night; and until the danger of attack had passed and the braves could take time to fish, the meals would always be the same: corn mush. To have taken along food for a midday snack, if only for the boy, would have indicated a weakness the Hurons regarded scornfully. Among the Hurons now, the Frenchmen had to live the Huron way.

The sun was straight ahead of them, low on the horizon and full in their faces, when at last the chiefs gave the signal that sent the canoes to shore. It was a relief to stand up, to stretch, to walk, but Isaac was careful not to luxuriate in his freedom of movement too openly, especially since the Hurons gave no hint of fatigue at all.

"Come on, Jean," Isaac said, "let's collect some firewood."

They made several trips into the woods, gathering far more kindling than was needed. When Isaac noticed that one brave was about to pull a log near the fire to sit on, he quickly went to help. Another Huron was down at the water, filling pots, and Jogues hurried to carry the pots back to the fires. The braves gave no sign that they were aware of him or that they welcomed his assistance, but he knew he should not expect that. When the mush was ready, he accepted his portion gratefully. It was tasteless, flecked with ash and soot, but it was filling and he was glad to eat it.

Now it was night. There was nothing more to do. The braves were settling around the fire, waiting for sleep. Isaac took Jean aside, just beyond the fire glow, and bedded him down and stretched out near to him.

"Say your prayers," Isaac said, adding, to avoid disturbing the Hurons, "to yourself."

He said his own prayers. He fell asleep.

2

The days were all the same. Up while the moon was still in the sky. Corn mush. Pack the canoes. Hour after hour after motionless hour. Beach. Make a fire. Help where possible. Eat. Sleep.

He wanted to read his breviary but had held off for two days because he feared the paddlers would feel he was disinterested in what was going on around him. The book was conveniently around his neck. On the third day he decided to try a little reading, part of him wary for any change in attitude among the braves. Sensing no change, each day he read a little more.

They reached the big island which Cartier had named Mont Réal. The river was swifter here, churning in crosscurrents. When the braves nosed the canoes to shore, pulled them out of the water and emptied them, Isaac realized that this was to be their first portage of the trip and that he must help. He said to Jean: "Carry a few pots." Jogues picked up his own effects and two bundles of supplies. It was a short portage, about two hundred yards, and in a half-hour they were back in the canoes. But in an hour they were ashore again, unloading, toting, loading, and this continued most of the day as they made their way over the rapids from the St. Lawrence into the Ottawa. That night Jogues was wearier and than he had ever been at the end of a day, and hungrier, and he slept better. On previous nights, sleep had been difficult, what with the mosquitoes that settled on him in clouds, the enormous flies that would not leave him alone, the crawling insects that got tangled in his beard and woke him in their struggles to escape. Sometimes Jean would touch him, weeping, frightened by the cry of some wild animal, and Isaac would say: "Don't be afraid, Jean, they don't come near because of the fires," but he spoke more in hope than in knowledge. He had wondered then how the Hurons managed to sleep so soundly, but now he was beginning to find out: they were exhausted.

The frequent portages of the next days seriously taxed the young Jesuit's endurance, and there were times when he could scarcely drag himself along. His main concern, however, was Jean Amyot. Weak from improper diet and insufficient rest, the boy had fallen ill, and it became necessary for Jogues to carry him over the portages. The paths were muddy, the rocks slippery, and often the way was steep. Jogues worried that, out of his own fatigue, he might drop the boy to his death in the rapids below. He knew Jean would be safer in the arms of one of the strong, sure-footed Hurons but, unable to speak the Huron language, he had no way to suggest it. Then an idea struck him. At the next portage, the priest moved quickly to a heavy bundle of hatchets usually carried by one of the Hurons in his canoe. With gestures, Jogues indicated that he would carry the cumbersome bundle if the Huron would carry the boy. The Huron understood and agreed and thereafter Father Jogues, bent under the heavy load, was nevertheless content that Jean was in more secure arms.

Now they came to the wide place in the river where the Island Algonquins lived. The Huron flotilla narrowed to a thin line in order to prevent too costly an ambush, should one occur. Here and there along the shoreline they saw a few Algonquins watching them, but there was no evidence of trouble. By nightfall they were beyond the islands, and Isaac noticed a new ease among the Hurons. Next morning, there was no rush to be on the way again. Some of the Hurons fished, roasting their catch in the morning fires. For the first time in two weeks, Isaac and Jean had a change in menu, and they welcomed it almost greedily. The Huron boys went swimming and Jean joined them. The priest went alone downstream and was able to bathe in the cold, invigorating river. When time came to resume travel, he was rested and refreshed. The day passed well, and so did the next and the next. Then they left the Ottawa and made a full day's portage across to Lake Nipissing. Jogues could tell that they were making good time. At Three Rivers, he had been told that the journey would take a month, and one of the Jesuits who had made the trip specified where Isaac could expect to find himself at the end of each week. The morning the canoes slid out into Lake Nipissing, the flotilla was a week ahead of itself.

The Hurons were pleased with their time and strove to improve it. That night they camped at the mouth of the French River, opening into Georgian Bay, and the next night they were more than halfway down the bay. The last morning, the nineteenth out of Three Rivers, the Hurons began to sing when they took up their paddles; each hour their song increased in vigor and joy. Isaac had to smile at the growing excitement; he felt it himself. At the hour when the sun was directly overhead, the leading canoes veered away from the shoreline and cut across the deeper, choppy waters of the bay toward the bluff on the southern horizon. Atop the bluff, Isaac knew, was Ihonatiria. An hour later, they were close enough for him to see the people on the shore, and a few minutes after that they were close enough to hear their song of welcome. The Hurons were home. And so was Isaac Jogues.

3

Charles Garnier and Pierre Chastellain were there on the beach, as was François Le Mercier, an older priest Isaac had known at Rouen. And Jean de Brébeuf. The Hurons had given de Brébeuf the name of Echon—he who carries the heavy load—and the name was fitting. As a seminarian, tuberculosis had almost forced him to give up his studies, and the fear was that he would never be able to carry his own weight, let alone heavy loads. But he had changed. He was now a towering man, broad-shouldered and big-chested, with the way of a mountain about him. He had been with the first Jesuits to arrive in New France in 1625 and he was among the first to return when the country was regained in 1633. He had spent all his time among the Hurons; he spoke their language as well as they did and he knew their minds as well as he knew his own. All the Jesuit rules for conduct among the Hurons had been written by him: he was the pioneer and the pace-setter. The Hurons respected him and they feared him. On treks, he could tote as much as any brave, without the least sign of fatigue. By himself he could carry a canoe on his shoulders, calling to those ahead to hurry along. In his dealings with chiefs, he was confident and forthright, respectful without being sub-servient, cooperative without being overly amenable. He knew that at any moment some piqued brave might sink a tomahawk into his skull, and he knew the surest way to make this happen was to let anyone think he was afraid it might happen. He was a born leader, a natural for the position he held as Superior of the Huron mission stations.

"You were a success on the journey," he told Isaac Jogues when they were all in the Jesuit cabin at the edge of the village. "I have already heard the braves speak well of you. Get ready to go on display."

"On display?"

"Everybody will be parading in here in a moment for a look at you."

Isaac laughed. "Lock the doors."

"The height of rudeness," de Brébeuf said, pretending to be shocked. "Lock a door on a Huron and he will burn your house down. They must be free to come and go as they please."

They began to come, women, children, old men, braves who had not been on the trip, entering without knocking, exchanging no acknowledgements, standing around, sitting around, glumly evaluating Isaac and Jean, taking in French conversations they could not understand, departing when they felt like it or remaining, if they chose, for the evening meal, in which they expected to share simply because they were present.

De Brébeuf said: "I hope you realize you have had your last private moment."

"I suspect so," Isaac admitted.

Garnier said: "It takes some getting used to. I've been here a month, but I still jump every time one of them comes strolling in."

"It is their way," said de Brébeuf.

Pierre Chastellain, also a month's veteran, said: "They don't expect you to knock at their house either. Just walk in."

Ihonatiria was considered a small village, with some five hundred people living in about thirty long narrow cabins. The cabins varied in size from twenty feet by ten to a hundred feet by thirty. The skeleton was made of slender trees and saplings; the siding and roof were bark, and there were holes in the arched roofs to permit escape for the smoke of the row of fires down the center of the building. At each end was an entranceway, usually covered with a strip of deerskin. Down each long wall ran a shelf, about a yard wide and four feet off the ground, on which the Hurons stored their food, supplies and clothes above the reach of rats and dogs. Each cabin housed as many people as it could accommodate, regardless of their family or personal relationships, and everybody slept on the ground. In summer, the cabins were hot, dark, musty and smelly; in winter, they were cold, dark, musty and smelly. Summer or winter, they were fertile breeding places for any diseases brought in by winds or wayfarers.

In comparison, the Jesuit cabin was luxurious. Fifty feet by eighteen, it was relatively new, having been built the year before by the Hurons, then improved by the four French laymen who worked with the priests as craftsmen, catechists and trek companions. The entranceway had doors, which, although meaningless to the Hurons, managed to keep out the dogs, most insects, and bad weather. At each end was a vestibule for supplies. The interior was neat and clean, the dirt floor rolled and pounded until it was like rock. The front half was the living quarters, and under the shelves each man had an assigned place to sleep. The rear half was the chapel, dedicated to St. Joseph.

Father Jogues asked: "Do many people come to Mass?"

"A few," de Brébeuf said, "but only out of curiosity."

François Le Mercier explained: "They have some strange notions about the True Presence. They figure that if Jesus died sixteen hundred years ago and we say now that He is present in our tabernacle we must have His corpse in there. Occasionally some of them get curious enough to come to Mass to try to get a look at it."

Isaac took the information with a philosophical nod. Charles Garnier said: "How clear that faith must be a gift, eh, Isaac?"

Jogues nodded again. "God will give it to them."

"We have much to do until He does," de Brébeuf put in.

The first thing Isaac had to do was learn the language. As he listened to it, he suspected that learning it was impossible. It was more of a cough than a language, spoken from the chest, all vowels, few consonants, no labials, and yet it was not a primitive language. With its complicated conjugations and declensions, it could be as subtle as French, as specific as Greek. An indicative feature of the Huron language was its lack of expression for abstractions and universalities. There was a word for good but no word for goodness, there was a word for knowing but no word for wisdom, there was a word for tender but no word for mercy. The people never experienced the abstract sensibilities and so they had never devised words for them. This presented a problem to the missionaries when they tried to express Christian characteristics to the Hurons, and it was one reason why they had won so few converts.

However, it was not the intention of the Jesuits to rush the Hurons into Christianity: even those who requested baptism were required to undergo a year's probation as catechumens. Only when death was near were exceptions made to this rule, and the rule was based on sound reason. The moral climate of a Huron village—or a similarly pagan village anywhere, for that matter—was so stormy with vice that the risk of apostasy by a few greatly outnumbered converts was discouragingly high. The Jesuits had observed this dangerous pattern in their missions in other parts of the world and had learned to avoid it. Experience showed that it was wise to progress slowly with prospective converts, until there were enough to provide strength to each other against the temptations that surrounded them. In the Huron atmosphere, rife with evil, the Jesuits could not hope to gather a steadfast nucleus of converts quickly; at best, they could lay the groundwork for future missionaries to build upon.

Thus, as Father Isaac Jogues began to study the Huron language, he was aware that fluency in it was no assurance that he would ever be able to persuade a single Huron to believe in his God, and he realized that merely trying to do so might well cost him his life. He was ready for that.

CHAPTER FIVE

1

A FEW days after Isaac Jogues arrived at Ihonatiria, he awoke one morning with a headache and a sore throat. His eyes hurt. When he tried to get up, pain shot through his body. He moaned. Father Le Mercier heard him and asked: "Are you all right?"

"I'm not sure," Isaac said. "I feel a little off." He tried again to get up but again the pain shot through him. He sank back in his cubicle under the shelf.

Le Mercier came over and knelt at his side and felt his forehead. "You are burning up."

Jean de Brébeuf noticed them. "Is there anything wrong?"

"He has a very high fever," Le Mercier said.

De Brébeuf stepped closer for a look at Jogues. "Maybe the journey was a greater strain on you than you realized. Take it easy for a while. Perhaps you should stay in bed today."

"I'll be all right," Isaac said halfheartedly.

"Yes, of course," said de Brébeuf, "but stay in bed today anyway." He glanced around for a quick study of the others and saw that Jean Amyot had not stirred. "What about you, boy?"

Jean struggled to open his eyes, but they fluttered shut. "I am not so well, Father."

De Brébeuf nodded, confident of his diagnosis. "Yes, it is the trip. You stay in bed today, too, Jean, do you hear?"

"Yes, Father."

"You will both be all right by tomorrow."

But they were not. Isaac's fever rose steadily and he began to cough badly. In the afternoon he developed nosebleed that would not stop. He was given soup but could not retain it. By nightfall he was so weak that even breathing required great effort. De Brébeuf was growing worried. He took Le Mercier aside and asked: "What do you think? Is it the influenza?"

"I'm afraid so," said Le Mercier. "The boy, too."

"If they picked it up on the trip, that means some of the braves might have it too." He studied Le Mercier for an opinion; Le Mercier nodded. "Can you do anything?"

Le Mercier shrugged. "The only medicines we have are purgatives. Isaac is so weak now I would be reluctant to give him anything like that. You know what he needs, don't you? He should be bled. It is the best way to break his fever."

"You would think that his nosebleed would be bloodshed enough," de Brébeuf said helplessly.

"I thought of that, but it doesn't seem to be working."

"Do what you can."

That night, Isaac's pulse was imperceptible. The fear of his death was in everyone's mind and showed in their eyes but nobody could mention it. Shortly after midnight, de Brébeuf went to the chapel and brought the Blessed Sacrament and gave Isaac what they all suspected was his last Communion. Later, Le Mercier knelt close and said: "Isaac, can you hear me?" Isaac parted his dry lips but no sound came from him. "Isaac, you must be bled. That's all that can help you. Will you permit it?" Nothing for a moment, then a flutter of Isaac's lashes: yes. Le Mercier looked around the room at the others. "Who shall do it?"

No one spoke. Each man looked at the other, each reluctant to take the sharp knife and cut the vein in Isaac's

[59]

arm, each aware that Isaac probably would not survive the ordeal.

Le Mercier asked again: "Who shall do it?"

Again there was silence.

Then, from Isaac: "I."

They moved him near the fire, where there was light, and they braced him by putting bundles at his back. They spread a cloth over his legs to protect his soutane and they held a pan to his chest and they rolled up his sleeve and they gave him the knife. He did not seem aware of what he was doing. His eyes were glazed, his breath was soft, with long moments between each gasp, and he stared blankly at the sharp knife as though he could not understand why in the world he was holding it. Then he looked at the vein, prominent in his thin arm. Slowly, disinterestedly, he put the knife to the vein and he made the cut.

There was a groan of pain from every man in the room except Isaac. He watched the blood pour from him and begin to fill the pan. When at last he looked up at the others there was a hint of disbelief on his face: this could not be happening. He fainted.

"Enough," Le Mercier said. He moved in with a bandage and bound the wound. De Brébeuf wiped Isaac's face with a damp cloth. Garnier and Chastellain carried him back to his cubicle and tried to make him comfortable. One of the laymen, François Petit-Pré, sat down close to Isaac to watch him. Then all the others, except Jean Amyot, who was moaning in his sleep across the room, went into the chapel to pray.

Early in the morning, Le Mercier glanced up from Isaac with a smile. "The fever is broken. He is still very sick, but he will be all right now."

"Thank God," said Pierre Chastellain. "But I am afraid, Father, that you now have a new patient." They all looked at him questioningly. He tried to grin, but the misery creeping through him caused his eyes to fill with tears.

"It starts," de Brébeuf said dismally.

Charles Garnier was making his annual retreat, spending his time apart from the others in the silence of his prayers, meditation and reading. He said to de Brébeuf: "Let me end my retreat. You will need me to nurse the sick."

"No, we'll manage," said de Brébeuf. "Besides, you have only a few more days to go."

But an hour later, while he was saying his Mass, Charles Garnier felt his sense of balance seep out of him, and before he was sufficiently aware of his condition to leave the altar he blacked out and fell to the ground.

It was starting among the Hurons, too. Within a few days the disease had invaded every long house in the village, striking people of all ages. News of outbursts came from other villages, from Ossossané, from Wenrio and Anonatea and Angwiens and Onnentisati. The epidemic was serious, and most serious about it was the fact that Jesuits, to whom the Indians always looked for help in such crises, were themselves in need of help. Two of the dozen Frenchmen at Ihonatiria—Father Pierre Pijart and the layman Simon Baron—were off on a trek and, from reports, seemed to be all right, but of those in the village only de Brébeuf, Le Mercier and Petit-Pré remained well enough to take care of the others. Chastellain sank lower than Jogues had been and was given the last rites. One layman became so weak that when his arm was cut for the bleeding there was not enough life in him to make the blood flow out.

Despite their own sickness, the Hurons were fascinated by the illnesses of the Jesuits and crowded into the mission cabin all day for a look. As usual, they entered without knocking. They wandered around peering into the faces of the sick Frenchmen, shouting across to each other when they noted anything interesting, and when they had enough of this they sat around the fires and smoked and discussed the whole thing. The Frenchmen themselves had no idea precisely what caused the influenza; they knew only that it was contagious and that recovery required rest, quiet, light meals and perhaps a bleeding or two. But the Hurons were certain they had the explanation. An angry spirit had caused the epidemic. All things had spirits—people, animals, fish, birds, trees, the grass, crops, the sky, water, clouds. Sooner or later the exact spirit would be revealed to somebody in a dream. It might be a beaver, angry because a brother beaver had been put to unnecessary pain in the process of being trapped, and the angry beaver-spirit had sent the sickness. To appease the spirit, to convince it to withdraw the sickness or perhaps to express its anger in another village, preferably the village of enemies, required the help of a sorcerer, a sorcerer who knew the dances and chants and sacrifices that could persuade the angry spirit to go away. Did the Frenchmen want the Hurons to fetch a sorcerer?

"No. No, thank you," said de Brébeuf. "We will manage. It would help, though, if you would leave us alone. The men should have quiet."

This was something the Hurons could not understand. When a Huron was ill, he sat up, his face pressed against his bent knees, a position which allowed his friends to dance around him in a circle while they wailed incantations to drive away the angry spirits. Some of the Hurons were now willing to give the sick Jesuits the benefit of this therapy, but Father de Brébeuf declined it.

"When a Frenchman is sick, he likes to lie down and be alone and try to sleep: that is our way," said de Brébeuf. "We prefer not to have too many people around us, noise makes us feel bad, and we feel worse when the room is so full of smoke we can't breathe."

Piqued, some of the Hurons left, but the others were unmoved by de Brébeuf's complaints and they remained where they were and as they were. This was particularly inconvenient at mealtime. Ordinarily, the Jesuits ate Huron-style: corn mush, whatever vegetables were left over from the harvest, whatever fish or meat was recently caught. But it was late September now, going into October, and the vegetables harvested in August were mostly gone, and there was available neither the time nor the men to fish or hunt. The Hurons would not think of offering to fish or hunt for the missionaries: a man should fend for himself. Nevertheless, when Le Mercier and Petit-Pré brought the food for the sick the Hurons who were in the cabin fully expected to be fed as well, and to refuse them would be an affront even worse than asking them to leave. This was not too bad as far as the corn mush was concerned, but figs and prunes and raisins were delicacies which the priests ate only on feast days or birthdays or when they were ill, and to be forced to share these with Hurons in good health, thereby depleting the supply faster, was both annoying and frustrating.

There was at least one good thing. Petit-Pré had found some autumn herbs still growing in this land where killing frosts and severe winter came so early, and he made a soup of them. The Hurons did not like the soup; they said it tasted terrible and after the first try they passed it up, which left more for the sick Jesuits. Also, the Jesuits had a hen, the lone survivor of a flock brought in the previous year. On irregular and unpredictable occasions, the hen produced an egg, which, in these days, produced a debate as to which of the sick men should get it. De Brébeuf was for killing the chicken in order to make a soup to nourish the sick a bit more tastefully, but he was discouraged by the realization that the brief luxury would mean the permanent end of egg production, however unreliable it was. He decided in favor of the eggs.

A brave in the village had trapped a live crane and was raising it. De Brébeuf went to him and tried to buy it, but the man resisted all offers. Finally the man said he had seen a deerskin in the Jesuit cabin he might accept in exchange for the crane. It was robbery, but de Brébeuf wanted the crane for the soup and he paid the price.

At last, Father Pijart and Simon Baron came back to Ihonatiria, both in good health. While traveling, they had heard about the sickness of the priests and changed their plans in order to hurry home. They were greatly needed and warmly welcomed. Their presence alone was enough to buoy the morale in the cabin where serious illness had raged for a month and still lingered. They went hunting and brought back geese and duck; these were caught while pausing on their migration to the south. Tracking a wounded deer took them near a small village where there were some surplus onions and potatoes to swap for part of the animal. And at mealtimes they stood outside the cabin door to engage Huron visitors in conversation before they could go inside and deprive the sick men of the food they so desperately needed.

Jogues was the first to recover. One afternoon he awoke from a nap without a pain in him. The relief sent joy through him and he tried to get up but he couldn't. That evening, however, he was able to sit up for his dinner and he remarked repeatedly how good it smelled and tasted. The next morning he was able to say Mass. He was a long time at his thanksgiving.

"Don't be in such a rush," de Brébeuf told Isaac when he presented himself for duty. "Stay around the cabin today; there is enough to do. Tomorrow, if you feel like it, you can try a walk in the village. In a couple of days you should be ready to go back to work."

There was work to be done. The epidemic still rampaged among the Hurons, taking scores of lives every day. There were people who needed treatment, others who needed baptism, others who needed burial.

And there was talk, ugly talk. The Huron mentality required an explanation for the epidemic, one which could be encompassed by the Huron superstitions of provoked spirits. Around the open fires in their long houses, the braves probed the question of responsibility for the sickness, the suffering, all the death. There had been sickness in the past but nothing like this, they all agreed, this was new in their land, and as such, they believed, it had to be caused by something—or someone—also new. At each fire, the discussion eventually came around to the same suspect: the newest Blackrobe, the one called Ondessonk. There had been no sickness before his arrival; he himself had been the first to be struck by it; surely he must have angered some spirit terribly to bring on such punishment. Having agreed upon their suspect, the Hurons next agreed on what they must do about him. As long as he remained in the village, the sickness would remain. Therefore, he would have to go, one way or another, before it was too late.

2

Almost a week passed before Isaac Jogues had enough strength to put in a full day. He was happy to be useful once again and he was only slightly troubled by the coolness with which many of the Hurons regarded him when he entered their cabins. De Brébeuf had heard the Huron gossip about Isaac and told him about it. De Brébeuf said: "They have to blame somebody for the epidemic, and you are it. They will forget it all when the epidemic is over."

"Am I in any danger?" Isaac asked.

"I don't think so. You won't be among friends for a while,

[65]

but then none of us are. Just carry on as though nothing is happening."

One by one, the French recovered from the attacks of the illness, and one by one the Hurons were falling victim to it. It was impossible to convince the Hurons to leave their sick alone. Dancing and chanting came from every cabin, all day, all night. To be of help, the priests had to fight their way through the circles of dancers and singers, brushing aside the clouds of smoke from fires, tobacco and the dusty floors. When death seemed near, the priests had to shout in order for the sick Huron to hear what they had to say about Jesus and Heaven and baptism. Practically all of the people who were baptized soon died, but those who rejected baptism were also dying, and this at least served to stem the growing Huron suspicion that baptism itself actually caused death.

One day Father de Brébeuf announced that since all the Jesuits were now well they should start visiting other villages to give what medical relief they could and to baptize those who wished it. He chose Isaac Jogues to go with him to Ossossané. News of their visit reached the village ahead of them and when they passed through the gate the people took one look at them and scattered.

"The sorcerers have been busy, I see," de Brébeuf observed. "Well, let's try our luck."

A brave stood at the door of the first cabin they approached. When they were within a few feet of him, he pulled a tomahawk from his belt and held it high, threatening. "Go away," he said, "go away. I don't want you to enter my cabin."

De Brébeuf pretended to be puzzled. "What is this? Why do you stop us? It is against the custom of your people to refuse a friend a place at your fire."

"You are not a friend," the brave said. "You have brought the sickness."

"You know better than that," de Brébeuf said patiently. "If we brought the sickness, would we give it to ourselves? We Blackrobes have had the sickness as bad as the Hurons. Ondessonk here was himself at death's door."

The brave frowned at Isaac. "I know this one," he said. "The sorcerers say the spirits do not want him here."

Isaac was about to speak, but de Brébeuf silenced him with a glance, then asked, "Have you had death in your house?"

"A woman and two men," said the brave.

"You say the sorcerers can appease the spirits. Why have they failed with this woman and the two men?"

"The sorcerers say the spirits are very strong this time."

"They were not strong enough to kill Ondessonk, and yet you say it is he they hate." De Brébeuf waited while the brave pondered this; then he said: "Are there any sick in your house now?"

"Yes. Many."

"Let us go to them."

The brave was uncertain.

De Brébeuf said: "Come now, you know me, my brother. In the past when there was sickness in your cabin, I and other Blackrobes came and chased it away. We can do so again. Ondessonk has his own weapon against the sickness, the weapon that saved his life. Let us go in to your sick and help them. The longer you keep us waiting here the less chance we will have to cure the people."

The brave was still unsure. Slowly he lowered his tomahawk, his evaluating glance moving from de Brébeuf to Jogues then to de Brébeuf again. Suddenly he turned and walked away, leaving the door to his cabin free.

"Let's go in," de Brébeuf said.

"Just a moment," Isaac said. "What is this weapon you said I have against the disease?"

"Bleeding. It worked for you, it should work for them."

"But suppose it doesn't work for them?"

"Then we shall have to think of something else. Meanwhile, we'll be getting to the dying and baptizing them. Come."

At first the people reacted violently against the idea of being bled. Cure a man by making his blood flow? Ridiculous. Then, on the third day, de Brébeuf was able to convince a woman to let Isaac bleed her dying teen-age son. Within a few hours the boy was greatly improved; by nightfall it was evident that he would recover. The incident was quickly the talk of the entire village and wherever Isaac went the sick held up their arms to him. He chose his patients carefully. Bleeding seemed dramatically effective upon those with high fever. The medical practice of bloodletting had been originated by Greek physicians who believed that most ailments were caused by an excess of blood, and in seventeenth-century Europe it was still practiced widely, either by incision or the use of leeches. No one knew why the treatment was sometimes effective—perhaps merely because of the removal of disease-bearing blood. It was somehow helpful at Ossossané.

But it was not helpful enough. The sorcerers, thriving on fear, had stirred the people against the missionaries. Councils were held at which votes were taken to determine the fate of the Jesuits. The vote was always the same: they must die. However, unanimity stopped there, for it could not be agreed upon when the priests should die or who should kill them. Braves appointed to the task refused out of the fear that perhaps the spirits friendly to the Jesuits might seek revenge. Chiefs who could have sent a mob against the priests gave thought to the profitable trading at Three Rivers and the risk of losing it, and the risk, too, that the French might send out armies of retaliation. However, the hesitation did not dilute the fear and hatred the sorcerers had aroused in the people at Ossossané, in every village. It would take only one wrong move, one wrong word, to spark an edgy brave to attack, and the priests knew it. Always alert, the Jesuits developed the faculty to perceive when someone was stealthily following them through the woods or through the pathways of a village, and they grew used to awaking in strange cabins to find someone standing over them. Nevertheless, they worked on, helping the sick, baptizing the dying, determined that if they themselves were to die they would die performing the holy purposes for which they had come here.

By the turn of the year, they had baptized over twelve hundred people. To the priests, the fact that almost all of these people died was no defeat. On the contrary, the battalion of souls sent to Heaven by baptism was a distinct victory. The only sadness was that there were not more, for many more had died. Ihonatiria was left with half its population by the end of February, and some of the smaller villages had suffered even worse. Time and again, the missionaries referred to the misfortune of their own illnesses early in the epidemic. Had they been well, they would have been able to save more of the Hurons, physically and spiritually. In this regret, they took solace in the confidence that the events of their daily lives were within the will of God, and although they wished some of the events had been different they accepted whatever happened to them as part of the Holy Design. They could only try to make the most of it, do their best with it, trusting that their results would be what God wanted.

Spring came, and with it came talk that the Hurons at Ihonatiria would give up their village this year and move elsewhere. The village was old by Huron standards, twenty or thirty years. The long houses were now beyond repair; the fields, farmed without fertilizer or irrigation, were producing smaller harvests every year. It was time to move on. The many deaths were another factor in the decision: the survivors of several towns agreed with those at Ihonatiria that it would be best if they all found a new place and built a new town and tried to start a new life.

The Jesuits had to make a decision about themselves. There were two methods of mission procedure. One was to assign priests to certain villages, usually the larger settlements, where they would live permanently, thus getting to know their people better and providing a stabilizing influence upon the community. The second method was for the missionaries to have their own headquarters, apart from any village, visiting all periodically for as long as necessary. Importantly, the second method afforded the missionaries the privacy they needed for spiritual exercises which would keep their vocations strong. Also, it freed them from affiliations with particular villages, which other villages might resent, and, as was now about to happen, it also freed them from the burden of having to pack up and move on whenever the people decided to do so.

Jean de Brébeuf preferred the first method, and because the mission group of which he was the Superior was small he felt they should all live in the same village. He chose Ossossané. The Jesuits were as despised at Ossossané as they were everywhere else, and it was only out of the hope that befriending the priests would result in richer rewards from the grateful French at Three Rivers that the chiefs of the village agreed to let them move in. Actually, they would not be in the village. A plot of land some one hundred yards away was awarded to them; the villagers would build the long house, a structure fifty by twenty feet.

"We would build a bigger house," said the great chief of Ossossané, "but we do not have enough hands for the work. You have killed too many of our people."

"I killed them?" de Brébeuf asked.

"Yes, when you sent the sickness to us."

To argue the point would have been useless; it was enough

that the missionaries would have a home. The work was begun in April and should have been finished in two or three weeks, but by the first of June the building was still little more than a skeleton. "They are not in a hurry to receive us," de Brébeuf observed. He assigned Le Mercier and Pijart to go to Ossossané and try to speed things along.

The Huron braves were now preparing for their annual trip to Three Rivers. Because of the epidemic, they had had little opportunity to hunt the previous winter, which meant they would have little to trade. Obviously, the forthcoming winter would therefore be another season of hard times.

The missionaries were busy at mail, writing letters the flotilla would carry to Three Rivers, letters which months later would finally arrive at France. Jogues wrote his mother a lengthy letter, carefully avoiding mention of his illness and the constant danger in which he lived. He wrote of the beauty of the country, the zeal of the priests, the customs of the people, the slow but steady progress of the missionaries, the need for prayers. Madame Jogues might not have learned of her son's true predicament had it not been for the fact that the offical report from the missions was published in Paris each year in volumes called *Jesuit Relations*. The books were widely read; they amounted to reports by foreign correspondents in a land that fascinated everyone. When Madame Jogues discovered what had actually happened to her son she wrote him a long letter, full of fear and cautions, but because of the distance between them another year had to pass before Isaac found out how worried about him his mother was.

As the departure day neared, chiefs of all the villages came to Ihonatiria to hold councils, to discuss the limit of the tribute they would pay the Island Algonquins and the prices they would demand for furs at Three Rivers. De Brébeuf, who, as the Jesuit Superior, attended some of the discussions, announced that he had written the priests at Three

Rivers, asking them to encourage generosity in the traders because of the hardships the Hurons had suffered and would suffer again this year. He also said that Pijart would accompany the flotilla in order to supervise the handling of missions supplies. Chances were, he also said, that more priests would be returning with the flotilla and he asked that the braves extend the same courtesies they had shown to other Blackrobes. The news was accepted without comment.

Then a surprising thing happened. The council had gone quiet, the chiefs and braves squatting around the fire smoking their pipes, waiting for anyone who had anything to say to speak his mind. A brave stood up. He was Tsiouendaentaha, who, at fifty, was considered an old man, but he had been a courageous warrior in his youth, an outstanding hunter, and he had often spoken with wisdom at previous councils. During the epidemic, his squaw had been baptized shortly before she died; he had been bled by Isaac and survived.

"I want to talk about the Blackrobes," Tsiouendaentaha began. "I know how most of my brothers feel about them, but I think there have been some misjudgments. It is said that the Blackrobes brought the sickness. I am old; I have seen many winters; I have seen the sickness worse then this year when I was a young man, long before the Blackrobes came to us. I do not believe what is said about them."

There was a stir of discomfort among the Hurons. Custom required that de Brébeuf should not display too much interest, but his heart was pounding. Tsiouendaentaha went on:

"I have seen other things. I have seen the Blackrobes take the food out of their mouths and give it to us when we were sick, even when they were sick and needed the food themselves. I have seen them sit up the whole night, putting the wet cloth to our brows when our faces were burning. I have

[72]

seen them make treks to far villages, in rain and in snow, because there was sickness or hunger in the villages and their help was needed. Enemies who stir evil spirits against us do not do these things. We do not do them ourselves, even for our own brothers."

De Brébeuf struggled to keep his gaze on the fire, which was the way the Hurons listened to each other at councils, and he did not look up until he heard Tsiouendaentaha say his name.

"Echon," Tsiouendaentaha said, "I have listened carefully to you and the other Blackrobes when you talked to the people about your religion and I remember it all. There is much I still do not understand, but I think all you say must be true. I have asked you many questions, Echon, you know that, and always you gave me answers, answers that grew out of each other, as the mountains grow out of each other as they stretch away to the horizon, and I have not been able to put these answers out of my mind. Since my squaw died, I have thought much on this matter, trying to decide when to go to you and tell you how I feel. I have chosen this council for it so that my brothers can hear what I have to say and so that they can join me, if they wish, in making you my brother, too. Echon, I ask you to give me the baptism."

De Brébeuf wondered what he would say if the chiefs indicated that he should speak, but no sign came. To himself, de Brébeuf was saying over and over: "Thank God, thank God, thank you, God." Tsiouendaentaha was the first Huron, freely and in good health, to ask for baptism. What a blessing that the first convert should be a man of such stature, a man with the courage to stand up and reveal his convictions at so important a council. Would this be the beginning to the Faith among the Hurons? Would it be the end of the danger? Would there be real friendship now; at least a tolerance?

Several silent moments passed. The chiefs got up and began to leave the council cabin. De Brébeuf looked over at Tsiouendaentaha to see if the Huron wanted to speak to him but there was no clue. The priest got up and left.

He could not have given happier news to his confreres then had he said the whole tribe had asked for baptism. For seven years the Jesuits had worked among the Hurons—seven years without a convert they could hope would live more than a few hours. To be sure, some they baptized on the brink of death had survived, but invariably these few ignored the fact that they were now Christians. That was the danger in it, but to try to pressure them into taking on Christian lives would be equally dangerous, for in their resentment there might be violence. And now here was Tsiouendaentaha, a respected man, an honored man, a good man. De Brébeuf could not remember ever having seen him indulge in the loose morality that rampaged in the village. And he had come forth on his own and offered himself.

"Grace, God's grace, we owe it all to God's grace," de Brébeuf said. "Here is a wonderful example of why we must all work harder, every minute. We can never tell when one word we say, one charitable deed we perform, will be just enough to open a man's heart to the grace to understand and believe."

Garnier asked: "When will you baptize him? You have said there should be a year's probation for a test of sincerity."

"I don't know," de Brébeuf said. "He certainly showed a lot of sincerity by what he did today. Let us wait and see. If he does not come here soon, I will go to him. It should not take long to find out how prepared he is."

Tsiouendaentaha came to the Jesuit house at the hour for the evening meal. He was silent and serious and took a place around the fire without giving any notice of the Frenchmen. When the food was ready, the Frenchmen lowered their

[74]

heads and made the sign of the cross and de Brébeuf led them in the prayer of grace. Tsiouendaentaha lowered his head and made the sign of the cross and listened. They began to eat, and the meal continued in silence for several minutes.

Finally, Tsiouendaentaha asked: "Echon, will you do it?"

"I will."

"When?"

"In good time." There were things de Brébeuf must find out. "Soon comes a big day for Christians, the day we honor the Holy Trinity. Do you know what the Holy Trinity is?"

"Yes. Our Father and His Son and Their Holy Spirit. I have heard you say it that way."

"That is the way it is said."

"I have heard you say that they live forever, but I cannot understand how this can be."

"Some things cannot be explained, but they must be believed."

"I believe it, then."

They went on this way, de Brébeuf introducing a Christian tenet, Tsiouendaentaha commenting on it. He had indeed listened well over the years and remembered well; he even knew some of the prayers.

At last, de Brébeuf said: "The feast day for the Holy Trinity is in four days. I will baptize you on that day, if you want it."

"I do."

"It is the custom that you should take a Christian name when you are baptized," de Brébeuf said. "I suggest that you take the name of Peter."

"All right."

The Frenchmen sitting around the fire smiled. How fitting that the first Huron convert should be named Peter: Petrus, the rock, the rock on which a new era could be built.

De Brébeuf said: "It is necessary for you to have a godfather, one of us, it will have to be, someone whom you wish to help you grow into a fine Christian. You may choose anyone you prefer."

Tsiouendaentaha frowned at this, but there was a hint of amusement at his eyes. He looked from one Frenchman to another, his gaze settling at last upon Simon Baron, the young layman. "You, will you accept as a son a man who has twice your summers?"

The young man grinned. "I shall be very pleased, Peter."

"So my father can take care of his son in my old age."

They were all very happy.

CHAPTER SIX

1

THUS THE first year Isaac Jogues spent among the Hurons came to a triumphant close. Peter's baptism was quickly the talk of the Huron nation. Many people came great distances to witness it. On Trinity Sunday morning, scores crowded into the small chapel which had been decorated with flowers and leaves and holy pictures. No one was certain what to expect; some of them thought that Peter, taking the white man's religion, would turn into a white man himself, and they were a little disappointed when he did not. The entire French community gathered around Peter as de Brébeuf said the prayers, asked the questions and applied the salt, holy oils and blessed water that were all part of the solemn ceremony. Then de Brébeuf said Mass, during which he gave Peter his first Holy Communion.

Afterwards, Simon Baron gave Peter a baptismal gift, a rosary, which Peter promptly put around his neck and vowed that he would wear forever.

"You must do more than wear it," Baron said. "You must pray it."

Peter said: "You must show me how, my father."

"I will, my son," said Baron, delighting in his new role. A few days later when the Huron fleet departed for Three Rivers, Peter was on the beach with the priests, raising his arm to give the farewell blessings. The Jesuits let him be: each Christian act he performed in public would give that much more encouragement to other Hurons thinking of following his example.

The new cabin at Ossossané was ready now. A work party came to Ihonatiria to pack the Jesuit equipment and carry it back. Because no definite decision had as yet been made about the future of Ihonatiria, de Brébeuf instructed Jogues and Le Mercier to remain there at least until the flotilla returned. All the others moved to Ossossané, including Peter, who said a son's place was with his father. At this early stage of Peter's new life, de Brébeuf thought it was a good idea. A brave and squaw, who had lost their son in the epidemic, offered to take Jean Amyot and raise him as their own. The boy, mixing easily with the Huron youths, had been more readily accepted by the village than the Blackrobes. De Brébeuf asked Jean how he felt about the offer; the boy was amenable, so de Brébeuf decided the arrangement would be made when the braves returned from Three Rivers.

The villages were now almost empty of their young men. Those who had not gone to Three Rivers were away in bands to seek better places to fish and hunt. Others went into the countries of the Petuns and the Iroquois to waylay lone travelers or to ransack small villages, this being a custom among all the tribes. At Ossossané, therefore, and at Ihonatiria and the other Huron villages they visited, the Jesuits were surrounded by women and old men and children. Isaac Jogues adjusted himself to what he felt would be a quiet summer. Two problems persisted. Influenza still lingered in the country, and so there were always patients. And the sorcerers, who were most influential upon the women and old men and the children, still ranted against the Blackrobes. In the villages were restless teenagers, on the threshold of their manhood when they would become braves, and they were unpredictable to the point where they presented serious dangers to the priests. Showing off, they would sometimes encircle a Jesuit as he made his village rounds, shouting at him, spitting at him, waving tomahawks at his head. It was difficult to decide how to treat them. Ignoring them made them more vicious; giving them attention only encouraged them. The Jesuits decided the best defense was to pretend the boys were merely bothersome, and so when the taunting began a priest would fling a glance that said, "Why don't you grow up?" And he would try to go on his way. When this failed, the priest had to decide which of the boys it was safest to brush aside, the boy least apt to react with violence. The incidents were always unnerving.

On the other hand, the women and the old men, disturbed by the warnings of the sorcerers, went sullen, refusing to have anything to do with the missionaries unless they were sick. This was frustrating, but at least it was peaceful. In the silent treatment was a unique opportunity: a priest could sit at a cabin fire and preach about Christianity to the women and the old men without interruptions, hopeful that some of his words and thoughts were having some effects.

By mid-August, sections of the Huron flotilla began to return, one of them bringing Paul Ragueneau. Now the four young men who had been ordained together—Jogues, Garnier, Chastellain, Ragueneau—were working together among the Hurons. The reunion was happily complete.

The returning flotilla brought other occasions for happiness. In response to de Brébeuf's appeal, the traders at Three Rivers had been generous with the Hurons, paying more than necessary for the few furs and pelts that had been collected during the epidemic and thus equipping the tribe better for the coming winter. And there was this: the Hurons told the Algonquins about the epidemic and blamed the Blackrobes for it.

"But how can that be?" the Algonquins had asked. "We

had the Blackrobes with us and we had no sickness. There was none at Quebec, either. You have made a mistake."

"It could be the one called Ondessonk," the Hurons suggested. "We never had the sickness so bad before he came."

"Ondessonk was here," the Algonquins pointed out, "and at Quebec, and we were not sick. Two other new Blackrobes went to you last year as well, you remember, and the blame for the sickness could be theirs as easily as Ondessonk's. No. You have made a mistake. The Blackrobes did not bring on the sickness. There is some other reason."

Thus when the flotilla returned to the Huron country, the braves admitted that they no longer blamed the Jesuits for the epidemic. Even when scattered outbursts of the disease continued to appear, the missionaries were free of suspicion, free to work. In this calmer atmosphere, the winter passed.

March brought a special triumph. Early in the winter, a man named Chihwatenhwa, the nephew of an important chief, caught influenza, and during the crisis, when he was at the point of death, he accepted baptism. He recovered. Well again, he soon left with other braves on the hunting that would produce the furs and pelts to be sold at Three Rivers, and he was away for several weeks. When he returned, he went to the Jesuit cabin outside the walls of Ossossané, and he asked de Brébeuf: "What do I do now?"

"About what?" the priest asked.

"When I was sick, you baptized me. That makes me a Christian, doesn't it?"

"Yes."

"Is that all there is to it?"

"No," said de Brébeuf. "There is a great deal more to it. You should have special instructions in the religion so that you can receive Communion. Your squaw and children should be baptized. You should be married in the Church. There is a great deal to do."

"Then let us begin."

In baptism, Chihwatenhwa had been given the name of Joseph, and now he insisted on being called that by everyone. He brought his wife, Aonetta, to the Jesuits for baptism, and she took the name Marie. Their children were baptized. Then Jean de Brébeuf celebrated the nuptial Mass for Joseph and Marie. Thereafter, the family came each day to the Jesuits for instructions for their first Communions, bringing along others who lived in their long house. Joseph had a quick and searching mind. During the catechism classes, he asked many questions, over and over, to be sure that others understood, as well as for his own satisfaction. By the time the Huron flotilla left on its 1638 trip to Three Rivers, Joseph was responsible for bringing two more Ossossané families into the Church.

Before the departure, the final arrangements were made to abandon Ihonatiria in favor of a low-lying site on the lake shore, several miles to the north. The manual labor of clearing the land was to be done by the women while the braves were away; later the braves would help the women complete the new long houses. All this would take months, and because of it Father de Brébeuf decided that the two priests at Ihonatiria, Jogues and Le Mercier, should be appointed elsewhere until the new village was ready to receive its missionaries. About twenty-five miles inland from Ihonatiria was the sizable village of Teanaustayaé, ruled by Chief Aochiati, one of the important leaders of the Huron nation. De Brébeuf's travels had previously taken him to the village, and he had promised the chief that one day he would appoint priests to Teanaustayaé. Now the time had come. Although the chief wanted the priests, custom required him to refuse de Brébeuf's first offer. Prepared for this, the Jesuit Superior took along gifts of hatchets, beads and cloth to be presented upon the refusal as a gesture of homage to the chief and in an effort to change his mind. The scene went exactly as custom prescribed, and after Chief Aochiati accepted both the gifts and the priests he displayed his own good intentions by giving the missionaries a long house in which to live.

The house was old and unused, on the verge of collapse, but it had an important significance. In the middle of June, when Isaac Jogues and Pierre Chastellain moved into it, Father de Brébeuf pointed out: "Not long ago, Chief Aochiati hated us. He actually sent some braves to Ihonatiria to kill us. Then the epidemic struck and we were able to come here to treat the sick. The chief has not forgotten that." He paused and glanced around the crumbling house, then he said: "Gratitude is not a natural Huron trait, but I believe that in giving us this house, the chief has shown a hint of it. This house, then, indicates that we are making progress. There was a time when we would not be given a place to get in out of the rain."

Isaac Jogues regarded the tattered roof. "Maybe we still haven't."

2

The first days were busy, with most of the time spent repairing the house. Although the villagers were interested enough to stand around and watch the work, few of them were inspired to help. It would have been unbecoming for Chief Aochiati to visit the house himself to see what progress was being made, but when he heard the Jesuits were having trouble stripping bark from the trees in sections large enough to patch up the roof properly, he ordered some young men to do it. A few girls were willing to bind leafy branches into brooms; boys were willing to tote the rubbish from the old cabin, hopeful that it might contain hidden treasure. Gradually the place became livable and in a week the Jesuits were able to take their first meal in it. Isaac Jogues said his first Mass in the chapel on June 25.

At unexpected moments, Chief Aochiati sent for de Brébeuf for the purpose of discussing religion. De Brébeuf always took Isaac along, usually deferring to him to answer the questions so that the chief would get used to the younger priest and thus be willing to continue the talks after de Brébeuf returned to Ossossané. There was no doubt of the chief's sincerity, and the only explanation for it, de Brébeuf felt, was in the answer to the prayers the missionaries had said for years for just such an opportunity to convert a tribal leader. Mission experience showed that once a leader was converted the people usually followed his example.

"Be patient," de Brébeuf advised Father Jogues one day when they were alone in their house. "Don't rush with him. He is an old man and he is set in his ways. His conversion would, of course, be a great help to us in working with the people, but if he should then fall away we would be worse off than ever. So go slowly. Be sure of him."

Knowing of the chief's interest in Christianity, the people were more willing to listen to Jogues and Chastellain as they went from house to house and sat at the fires to talk about religion. Sometimes a brave would ask a question; occasionally there would be a brief group discussion, but there were no signs that anyone was being won over. This was to be expected. A conversion would have required a complete change from the Huron way of life; habits, attitudes and traditions which had been bred in the people for centuries would have to be abandoned. The personal convictions necessary for a Huron to make such a change could not be easily inspired in a few weeks, even a few years, and the Jesuits were aware of that.

One of the old traditions was already threatening the Jesuit work at Teanaustayaé. Village leaders had decided that the time was propitious to renew the tribe's feud with the Iroquois. Every night, medicine men stirred the people with eerie chants and wild dances; every morning, war parties headed south to the Iroquois country, attacking hunters, burning isolated long houses, plundering small villages. Their bloodthirsty passions aroused by their victories over their powerful enemy, the people were deaf to Jesuit arguments that the unprovoked attacks were wrong, and even Chief Aochiati brushed aside the missionaries when they tried to persuade him to put an end to the terror. This was precisely the kind of relapse into the old tribal ways that Father de Brébeuf had warned the younger priests to expect, and he knew now that nothing would stop the Hurons until either their fury was spent or the Iroquois retaliated with their superior strength.

One day a band of Teanaustayaé warriors brought back a prize: eleven Iroquois prisoners, members of the Oneida tribe. As they were led through the gate, a great cry went up from the Hurons, the same savage cry of vengeance Isaac Jogues had heard at Three Rivers when the Algonquins first sighted the two Mohawk prisoners. And the same fury occurred. The Hurons fell on the Iroquois, biting them, kicking them, stoning them, beating them with burning branches.

"Look," Father Chastellain called, pointing. "Aochiati."

The chief had come out of his house and, surrounded by his advisors, watched the chaos with an expression of stern pride upon his face. He gave an order to his advisors, and three of them went forward to the crowd to carry it out. Men and women began to break away from the crowd, some of them to start erecting a platform in the village clearing, others to rush outside the gates to collect kindling in the forest beyond.

When Jean de Brébeuf realized what was happening, he exclaimed: "Dear Lord! Aochiati is going to burn them!"

A moan of despair came from Isaac Jogues. "Can't you stop it?"

"We can do nothing."

Pierre Chastellain turned to go. "I cannot watch this," he said.

"Wait here," de Brébeuf instructed; then he hurried away, rounding the barbaric mob, to Chief Aochiati. The two young priests watched their Superior plead with Aochiati briefly, then saw the chief nod, and de Brébeuf came back to them. "The chief is willing to let us baptize the Iroquois, if they want it," he said. "Isaac, fetch the baptismal kit from the house, quick."

Moments later, when Jogues returned to the clearing, he saw that the platform had been completed and the Iroquois prisoners had been placed on it. De Brébeuf was with them, and as Isaac approached he could hear the priest urgently saying:

"You will all be dead in these fires in a little while, you know that. But these fires will hurt you just a short time. There is another fire, however, that burns all night and day, every day, forever, and that fire awaits the wicked man after death. My brothers and I have come here to save you from that fire. The Great Spirit had promised that if you let us pour these waters on you your sins will be forgiven and He will take you into His house after your death and there will be good things for you through all the days of the world. He wants you to do this. He Himself died a death worse than yours so that you could escape the fires that burn forever. He loves you. Even though you do not know Him, He is your brother and your father. He has sent us here from our homes, far away, in order to tell you this." Intently, forcefully, de Brébeuf went on, explaining as briefly but as thoroughly as he could why the doomed men should be baptized. Then: "Do you wish it to be done?"

[85]

The young leader, his scalp sliced away from his skull, spoke. "Yes."

"And you believe what I have said?"

"We are already dead men. Why should you lie to us? What would you gain from it? If this is so important to you that you have come here from your distant homes, even here on this platform in front of the people who would kill you as easily as they kill me, it must be true. I believe you." He turned to his men. "You must believe, too." They indicated that they did.

De Brébeuf said: "Pierre, Isaac, now. Quickly."

The three priests began to baptize the eleven Iroquois. Behind them they could hear the murmuring crowd, anxious, impatient, angry. When the priests finished and left the platform, Aochiati gave the signal and the crowd pushed forward.

Chastellain was a few steps ahead of his two confreres when they reached the edge of the clearing on the way to their house. De Brébeuf said: "Wait. These are our first Iroquois Christians. We ought not to let them die alone." He turned around, facing the crowd; Jogues and Chastellain stepped to his side. As de Brébeuf began saying the prayers for the dying, the two young priests joined him. As they prayed, they watched, and they could not believe what they were seeing.

Four of the Iroquois were already dead, their heads split open by tomahawks. Screaming women now dragged them from the platform and held them over the bonfires. The air went thick with the smell of roasting flesh. One by one, the Iroquois on the platform fell under the Hurons' hatchets. Legs and arms and heads were handed down to the mob and hurried to a fire.

Now only the leader remained, twisting, squirming, fighting. He grabbed firebrands from his tormentors and threw them back. The howling Hurons crushed down on the man, overpowered him, and they threw him off the platform into a fire. He struggled to his feet and, picking up burning wood, ran into the crowd. Stunned, the crowd parted, opening a passage.

The Iroquois ran down it to the palisade wall and held the burning wood against the dry fence in an effort to set fire to the village. With a roar, the Hurons rushed to the fence and beat out the fire, and they threw the man to the ground and chopped off his hands and feet. Boys picked him up and carried him back to a fire. His body jerked and wiggled as the flames enveloped him. The boys could not hold him: they let him drop into the fire. He rolled over and crawled away on his elbows and knees. The crazed mob bellowed, hooted and wailed. A big burning log was pushed forward, over the man's legs and onto his chest. He squirmed from under it and started to crawl again. A Huron brave with an ax came near and sank it into the man's neck, again and again, until the head rolled away. The body trembled and twitched, than sagged into lifelessness. A great victory cheer went up as the crowd collected the pieces of the man and took them to the fires.

The three Jesuits went to their house and for the rest of the day they scarcely spoke to each other. At night they crawled into their cubicles, but they could not sleep. All night they lay awake, listening to the deep and heavy sighs that came first from one priest and then another. All night they heard the songs and drums of the Hurons in the clearing as they feasted on the bodies of the prisoners. From time to time there were noises at the door, but the priests did not bother to investigate. In the morning, they saw that the bones of the Iroquois had been tossed into the house.

"Is it a warning?" Chastellain asked.

"More an act of scorn," said de Brébeuf. "Somebody apparently thinks that in baptizing the Iroquois we took

[87]

their side. Throwing the bones in here is, I suppose, meant to put us in the same low, vanquished category."

"It is a compliment, then," Isaac Jogues said. "I have never seen such courage."

They gathered up the bones and buried them in their chapel.

3

That summer there was a change in the Jesuit command. In August, Father Jerome Lalemant arrived with the main body of the Huron flotilla. He presented documentation from Paris which made him Superior of the Huron mission, replacing de Brébeuf. This was a facet of religious life that was sometimes puzzling but always stabilizing. One day a man might hold a position of power and influence; the next day, he might be assigned the position of doorkeeper. The periodic reassignments did more than give new men a chance at leadership: it reminded each man that he was not working for himself but for the Society and that any position within the Society was worthwhile, wherever it put a man, whatever it required him to do. The stability in this was that it assured humility, for without humility, without the suppression of pride and ambition for the sake of the common good and the service of God, the entire nature of the religious life would be distorted and its goals would be seriously endangered.

De Brébeuf welcomed the change. The growing number of Jesuits in the Huron country had turned him into more of an executive, limiting his direct contact with the people because of his increasing responsibilities to his men. Now all that would end, now he could return to what he wanted to be—an ordinary missionary, out in the bush, up to his heart in village affairs.

Lalemant announced sweeping changes. He favored the mission approach which provided a permanent headquarters for the priests, from which they could make their regular treks to the villages. He hoped to build such a headquarters within a year at a place apart from the villages, a place of quiet and privacy where the priests could periodically revitalize themselves spiritually. There was wisdom in this. Even the best missionary could, out of time, habit and environment, become lax, if only to the extent of neglecting his prayers. A missionary's deep spirituality was, therefore, his life's blood. Without it, he lost his purpose; without it, he was something more than a philanthropist but something considerably less than a priest. To safeguard their spirituality, Lalemant issued a new regimen.

The idling of unoccupied Hurons in the mission longhouses was to be discouraged, Lalemant instructed. The habit merely condoned loafing and tied up priests who could otherwise be out at work. Henceforth, only Hurons on mission business were to enter the houses during the day and only Christians could enter during the hours the doors were barred, from five o'clock in the evening until eight in the morning. The priests were to arise at four for meditation, prayers, Mass and breakfast before opening the doors. One priest was to remain in the house each day, serving as catechist and infirmarian while the others worked in the village or traveled to nearby villages. Lunch was at two, with Bible-reading during the meal; Christian Hurons could be present. After the doors were closed at five, the priests were to spend an hour and a half at study and conferences until dinner, and dinner was to be taken in silence while someone read from a spiritual book. The last hour of the day, from eight to nine, was reserved for night prayers, examination of conscience and preparation for the morning meditation.

As confining as the schedule seemed, it nevertheless

[89]

proved rewarding and productive. The priests had grown up on similar schedules in seminaries and while teaching, and they knew that an organized day offered more opportunities to get things done than the scatter-shot efforts to which they had been forced to resort as a result of allowing themselves to be at the beck and call of the Hurons. Also, they were happy to have their spiritual exercises set at definite hours: now there was less risk of letting oneself get so busy at other affairs that there was no time to pray, or at least not enough time to pray properly.

Lalemant also took immediate steps toward the construction of the new headquarters. He chose a site on a creek which emptied into an inlet of Georgian Bay, conveniently halfway between Ossossané and Teanaustayaé. It was to be a fort, like the one at Quebec, barricaded for privacy as well as protection, and when completed it would include a church, a rectory, a guesthouse for Hurons, a workshop, a hospital and a catechist school. The approval of the Huron chiefs was necessary before the mission-fort could be built. At a council of chiefs in March, 1639, Father de Brébeuf won their approval, and he also reached agreement on the amount of wampum to be paid the Huron construction workers. The total amount was more than the Jesuit budget afforded. Therefore, that summer, in their homeland, all the Jesuits begged their relatives and friends for donations. They pointed out that most of the big European cities had started this way: first a mission-fort, then outside the walls the homes of converts who wanted to live near their priests, then a trading-center for the countryside, then a village, a town, then a city. It could happen here, the Jesuits predicted.

To a degree, the evolution was well under way. Three more Jesuits had arrived with Lalemant in 1638. One was Antoine Daniel, the priest who, worn and weary after four years among the Hurons, had returned to Three Rivers when Isaac was there. He had regained his health and asked to be reassigned to the Hurons. The other two were newly ordained, fresh from France, Simon Le Moyne and François Du Peron. No missionaries arrived during 1639, the year the fort was built, but the following summer the fort was ready and welcomed two more newcomers, Pierre Chaumonot and Joseph de la Reviere, and with them came more lay volunteers. That autumn, when Lalemant sent out orders that all missionaries should move to the fort, there was a French population of twenty-seven—thirteen of them priests—and already the Hurons were beginning to look to the fort as a center for trade and medical treatment.

During the last weeks before moving to the fort, Isaac Jogues was put in charge at Teanaustayaé, assisted by Paul Ragueneau and Simon Le Moyne. Chief Aochiati knew the Blackrobes would soon be leaving. He sent for Isaac. "Will you never come back, Ondessonk?" he asked. "Are there to be no more Blackrobes in my village?"

"The Blackrobes will come to your village for as long as you want them," Isaac assured. "The only change will be that the fort will be our home, and when we come here or to other villages we will stay just a few weeks. In this way, we will be able to visit many villages and do more good."

"It will not be the same, not having you here all the time," the chief said.

Jogues said: "Whenever you need one of us for any special purpose you have only to send a message and we will come."

The chief thought a moment, then he said: "I have a special purpose now, Ondessonk. Will you baptize me before you leave?"

Isaac was not surprised. Of late, Aochiati had sent for him frequently and they had long talks about religion. Although Aochiati did not attend Mass himself, he permitted

[91]

his people to do so. Several of them had recently begun instructions, presumably with his tacit approval. However, still vivid in Isaac's memory was the massacre of the Iroquois. He could remember Aochiati standing there, arrayed in his finery, goading his people on, giving the orders to build the fires, then sending the mob in for the kill. De Brébeuf had said Aochiati might well be a prospect for conversion because of the friendliness he had at first displayed, but after the massacre Jogues seriously doubted it, and even now, over a year later, he still doubted. Elusively, he asked: "Do you really want to be baptized?"

"I have asked for it," Aochiati declared.

"You would have to give up many things," said Isaac.

"I am an old man," said the Chief. "There is not much left for me to give up. But if you say so, I will give up tobacco in order to be baptized."

For a Huron, this was like offering to give up food. Isaac said: "You will have to take instructions."

"For how long?"

"A year."

"I may not live a year."

"It is the rule," Isaac said. "Of course, if it appears that you may die before the year has passed we will baptize you, just as we baptize all the dying who request it."

Aochiati regarded the priest sadly. "You do not trust me, Ondessonk. And I know why. This thing you dread, it has not happened again, has it?"

"No," Isaac conceded, "but the Hurons have not been on the warpath since then."

"As long as I live, my village will never go on the warpath."

Father Jogues tried not to show his astonishment. This was a remarkable statement from a man whose life's career had been war. Jogues asked: "What has led you to this decision?"

"The things you have said, Ondessonk, and what Echon said many times before you, that a man should not kill except in self-defense."

Isaac did not know what to say. His year in the village had made him wary of the chief's unpredictability: one day the man could be a saint, the next day a savage. It was true that recently there had been peace in the village and the priests were free to do their work; it was also true that Jogues had never heard Aochiati sound as sincere as he did this moment, but still the priest had his doubts.

The chief asked: "Well, Ondessonk?"

Isaac tried a new tack. "A great chief who is a Christian would not allow sorcerers in his village."

"I will send mine away."

"And he would not believe in the evil spirits any longer."

"I do not believe in them now."

"He would persuade his people not to believe in them."

"I will do what I can."

It was all a man could expect. Isaac said: "I will give you my answer in the morning." This was the Huron custom, pondering a decision overnight, and Aochiati accepted it.

As he walked back to his cabin, Jogues pondered the decision he had to make. The missionary policy had been: When in doubt, don't, and Isaac had his doubts. But at what point did a decision like this pass out of a priest's hands into God's? A priest could not read minds; he could only take a man's word. God alone knew the full truth. This was true in the confessional, at a deathbed, at a baptismal font. As for the change in Aochiati that Isaac had trouble believing, well, had there not been the Good Thief at Calvary? Had there not been a Mary Magdalene? Had there not been, for that matter, a Peter Tsiouendaentaha at Ihonatiria and a Joseph Chihwatenhwa at Ossossané? These two Hurons, raised in the same environment as Aochiati,

[93]

once participating in his cruelties and vices, were now both model Christians. So it could be with Aochiati. But Isaac still felt uneasy. He wished there would be a sign, but he dared not ask for it.

He opened the door of the long house, and as he entered he recognized a familiar face in the shadows of the fire. "Joseph Chihwatenhwa!" he exclaimed. "I was just thinking about you. What brings you here?"

"Chief Aochiati sent word for me to come here," Joseph said. "He says you are going to baptize him and he wants me to be his godfather."

Was this the sign? Isaac asked: "What do you think, Joseph? Do you believe the chief would make a good Christian?"

"I have been praying that God would give him the grace to want to be," Joseph admitted.

"I think your prayers are about to be answered," Isaac said. "God's grace is all anyone needs, and apparently He has given it to Aochiati."

A week later, when Isaac arrived at the new fort, he was able to report the important baptism. There was great interest in it. Aochiati was the first great-chief to enter the Church. Who could tell what might grow out of his conversion? The conversion of the entire village, perhaps. Of the entire clan. Of the entire tribe. Of the entire Huron nation.

It was too much to hope, so early in the Huron mission years, but it was not too much to expect of the future. God had forever.

4

It was a time to grow.

In September, 1639, the fort was dedicated to the Blessed Virgin and called Fort Sainte Marie. Hereafter, Lalemant announced, the men would be spending most of their summers at Sainte Marie. Summers were quiet in the Huron country, with most of the men away fishing, scouting, trading. Summers, then, the Jesuits would gather at Sainte Marie to make their annual retreats, to refresh their vocations with prayers, study and community life. Winters, the men would make their treks to villages assigned to them, staying out for several weeks at a time, then returning to Sainte Marie to replenish their supplies and themselves for a few days before starting out again.

But this winter would be different. "We need some statistics," Lalemant said. "If we are to make long-range plans, we must have some idea of the problem ahead. We have no idea how many Hurons there are. We have little contact with the Nipissings to the north, less with the Petuns to the south, and all we know about the Chippewas and the Ojibwas to the west is that they are there. So I propose that we spend the winter taking a census and obtaining material for accurate maps."

He gave the assignments. Isaac Jogues and Charles Garnier were given the longest trip—to the Petuns. Until now, the only white man to go among the Petuns was Jean de Brébeuf, who had penetrated the Petun fringes in 1625. Although the Petuns were part of the Huron federation and had intermarried with the Hurons, they ordinarily kept to themselves on their wide peninsula between Lake Huron and Lake Erie. The scant news of them was all bad. Only the narrow Niagara River separated them from the Iroquois, so they were frequent victims of attacks by their traditional enemies. They had lost many braves in the epidemic. This summer, a long drought brought on a famine, causing more deaths and hardship.

De Brébeuf told Isaac: "Joseph Chihwatenhwa has relatives among the Petuns. I suggest you stop off at Ossossané for any advice he may have for you."

On November 1, the Feast of All Saints, the Jesuits filed out of Sainte Marie on their journeys. By nightfall, Isaac and Garnier were at Ossossané, in Joseph's house, listening to his words. "You will not have an easy time," he warned. "The people have suffered much and they blame you."

"Why us?" Garnier asked.

"They heard the talk against you by the Hurons, that the Blackrobes brought the epidemic. So they blame you, too, because they had no rain."

The same old story. Isaac said: "Maybe your relatives will welcome us because we know you. Where is their village?"

"I will show you the path in the morning. The village is three days' walk," said Joseph, "but my relatives may not be there. Their village has lost many people. Chief Aochiati has sent word there that the people can spend the winter at Teanaustayaé and he will give them food and protection."

"That is very good of him," Isaac said.

"He is a Christian now and knows what he must do."

Next morning, Joseph led the two priests to the Petun trail and walked with them for several hours. Snow covered the ground and they could not make good time. Before parting, the three men prayed together for a safe and successful trip. Then the two Jesuits were alone in the wilderness.

The trip was neither safe nor successful. For almost four months, Isaac Jogues and Charles Garnier wandered aimlessly through the Petun country. At most villages they were refused entrance; at others the Petuns were sullenly arrogant. There was no opportunity to evangelize, little opportunity even to converse. Joseph's relatives were curt. "Chihwatenhwa is no longer one of us," they said. "He has given up his people for your religion and we have no more duty to him." The priests were allowed to remain the night, but first thing in the morning they were ordered to leave. It was that way everywhere. In villages where they were permitted inside the gates they were nevertheless kept out of long houses, and so most nights they slept outdoors, huddling against the warm sides of buildings to ease the freezing cold. Usually they had to pay for food with beads and trinkets.

In January they heard of a village where there was sickness and they went there, but only because of the lethargy in the village were they allowed to enter. They treated the patients the best way they knew, by bleeding them, and several of them recovered. But the people were not grateful. Instead they said the Blackrobes had effected the cures with the help of their evil spirits, and even those who recovered were sorry they let the Blackrobes touch them. The Blackrobes ought to be killed. A council was held to arrange it.

The hope that the familiar danger would pass, as it had passed before in other places, encouraged them to stay one more night, but when they went to the house where they had been sleeping they were forbidden to enter. The meaning was clear: custom required that a man in whose house an enemy died was obliged to destroy the house to prevent the dead enemy's spirit from haunting it.

"We'd better go," Garnier said.

"Yes," Isaac agreed. "I wish we could go back into the house for a minute to get our packs."

"I don't think we ought to try," Garnier offered.

They waited until there was no one near the gate, then they left quickly. It was night and very cold. They stumbled onward in the darkness for about an hour when they both became aware that someone was following them. To try to elude an Indian at night in the woods was foolhardy. Jogues gave a signal and the two priests left the path and hid behind a tree. They could tell that their pursuer had paused, waiting surely for the wind to bring the scent of them. Then:

"Ondessonk?"

The voice was familiar. Isaac tried to place it. "Joseph?"

"Yes, Ondessonk."

"Thank God!" He stepped from behind the tree. "You must be my guardian angel. You are always near when I need you."

Joseph said: "I saw my relatives at Teanaustayaé and they told me what it was like for you here. I thought you might need me."

"We do."

Garnier asked: "How did you find us?"

"All the Petuns know where you have been every day."

"But how did you find us tonight?"

Joseph pointed to the footprints in the snow. "Who else in this country wears shoes?"

They laughed and were surprised to find themselves doing it.

"We can go back to the village," Joseph said. "It will be all right now."

They remained in the Petun country three more weeks, gradually working their way back north to Sainte Marie. Receptions were no warmer than they had been, but now at last, with Joseph along, they were safe, and the two priests were able to complete their census. They were also able to preach a little, with Joseph serving as interlocutor, asking the questions he knew were in the Petun minds. And, again due to Joseph, they were able to baptize some of the dying they encountered. Back at Sainte Marie in February, Isaac prepared his report of his journey. From such reports by his men, Father Lalemant was able to calculate that living in approximately two hundred and fifty villages of the Huron federation were some fifteen thousand people, of whom perhaps thirty were dependable Christians, a small percentage but a hopeful size in view of the fact that most of the conversions had occurred in the past year. Lalemant felt the missionaries had reached the turning point. From now on, he was confident, things would go better.

[98]

That spring, Isaac Jogues wrote home: "I am a house-keeper now. Father Superior has put me in charge here at Sainte Marie. I see to it that the meals are properly prepared, that the buildings are kept clean, that the vegetable gardens are tended, that the construction work goes on. Strange life, this, for a missionary."

To avoid worrying his mother, he carefully evaded mentioning what type of construction was going on. On three sides of the fort and about a hundred and fifty feet from the palisade, a wall of brick and stone was going up, and a broad moat was dug on the side that faced the river. The reason: The Iroquois were on the warpath. Armed with muskets obtained in trading with the Dutch and English, they were crossing north into the Huron and Algonquin territory, brazenly attacking villages, caravans and flotillas. The colonial authorities at Quebec considered the threat to be so serious that Father Le Jeune was sent to Paris to plead with Cardinal Richelieu for funds to build a fort at the mouth of the River of the Iroquois, which emptied into the St. Lawrence midway between Montreal and Three Rivers; the money was granted and the work begun. Even so, the scattered Huron and Algonquin villages were defenseless against the Iroquois. Despite brave efforts to hold back the Iroquois onslaughts, the unarmed Huron and Algonquin warriors were routed again and again, and there was no telling when the Iroquois would stop. Isaac's new assignment at Sainte Marie, therefore, was not as hollow as he made it sound. Upon the speed and skill to which he goaded his Huron workers could well depend the survival of the mission-fort itself.

Adding to their growing fears was the murder of Joseph Chihwatenhwa. That winter he had accompanied two Jesuits on a census-taking trek to the eastern regions of the Huron country, and while passing through treacherous waters his canoe sideswiped some sharp rocks and was torn.

After skillfully bringing the damaged craft to shore, Joseph suggested that the two priests remain at the river while he went into the woods to find large trees which he could strip for the bark to make a new canoe. He was gone a long time. Worried, the two priests went to look for him. When they found him, he was already dead, and he had been scalped. Still piercing his chest was a broken lance of the type the Iroquois used. To the Jesuits, Joseph's murder could be considered a martyrdom because he had died while working for the mission, but to the Hurons the death was primarily a warning of how deep the Iroquois had penetrated into their country, and there was a new terror in the land.

That summer, de Brébeuf was chosen to escort the 1641 flotilla to Three Rivers, and Lalemant ordered him to remain there a year to rest after his difficult winter at census-taking. The Hurons themselves were not too anxious to make the trip this year because of the Iroquois dangers, but when they learned that Echon would accompany them their fears were somewhat abated. Echon, they believed, could do anything; Echon would get them through. The flotilla left, and it was not until late August, when the traders returned, that Jesuits could relax, knowing that Echon had indeed got them through without incident. Even the most optimistic Jesuit had had his doubts.

Meanwhile, an opportunity arose for the Jesuits to make contact with the Indians far to the west. The Ojibwas, who lived along the rapids that linked Lake Superior and Lake Huron, were to hold their feast for the dead in October, the feast at which they paid tribute to their warriors of the past who had died valiantly in defense of the tribe. By custom, other tribes at peace with the Ojibwas were invited to attend. Both the Hurons and Algonquins were sending delegations, and the Hurons invited the Blackrobes to go along. No Frenchman had been among the Ojibwas since the explorer Jean Nicolet, in 1634, and Father Lalemant looked upon the invitation as a good chance to renew the relationship, anticipating the day when there would be enough Jesuits in the New World to assign some to the western tribes. He appointed Isaac Jogues to accompany the Huron contingent; Father Charles Raymbault, a veteran of five years in the Montreal area, would accompany the Algonquins.

In late September, the two groups met where the French River entered Georgian Bay and they began the journey of three-hundred and fifty miles to the Ojibwas. Once again, Isaac witnessed the enormousness, the majesty, of the New World, the great lakes stretching away in all directions like oceans. The thought was staggering: here in this broad, beautiful, magnificent land were, surely, thousands upon thousands of people who had never heard the name of Jesus Christ. What a task, what a challenge, what an opportunity lay ahead for the missionaries yet to be born who would come here, and slowly, gradually but steadfastly plant the Faith until there was not an acre without a Christian soul.

The trip took eighteen days, a long trip for just the scheduled week's visit to the Ojibwas, but, as it turned out, worth every moment. The Ojibwas and their neighbors, the Chippewas, were overwhelmingly hospitable and friendly, pledging brotherhood and peace to the Blackrobes and pleading with them to remain. The two priests were invited to preach, to explain their religion, and they were urged to baptize the old and the sick. A month later, back at Sainte Marie, Isaac was able to report to Father Lalemant that a rich harvest of souls awaited any missionaries who could go immediately to the tribes along the western lakes. As tempting as the opportunity was, the Jesuits were committed to the Hurons and could not abandon them merely on the promise of greater success elsewhere.

The winter passed. In April, 1642, Lalemant summoned Isaac Jogues to his office and told him: "I have chosen you

[101]

to go with the flotilla to Three Rivers this year. Are you willing?"

In Jogues's view, his Jesuit vow of obedience answered the question for him. "I will do whatever you say."

"It will be dangerous," Lalemant pointed out. "I have reports that Iroquois war parties have been seen all along the route. You are free to refuse, if you wish."

"I shall go."

Father Lalemant accepted the decision with a nod, as though he were expecting it. "Some of the chiefs think things will get worse when summer comes."

"So I have heard," said Isaac. "But the trip must be made."

The chiefs did not think so. In May, several of them arrived at Sainte Marie to hold a council regarding the trip, and they announced: "We have decided not to go to Three Rivers this year. The Iroquois have killed too many of our braves; those we have must stay home to protect the villages and rebuild the long houses that were burned in the attacks."

"But what about fresh supplies and equipment?" Lalemant asked. "How will you be able to get through the winter?"

"We have very little to trade this year," one chief said. "There was no time to hunt last winter. The furs we have are not worth the trip. We will just have to get along somehow and hope that next year will be better."

The Jesuits could not put off the trip that easily. Mission supplies—medicines, wheat, sugar, dried fruit, building equipment, cloth, wampum—were low, as they always were this time of the year, and without replenishment the priests could not possibly get through the winter. Moreover, there were the annual reports that had to be in Quebec in time to be transshipped to Paris. There were, too, Huron children at the Quebec school to be brought back; there possibly was a priest or two at Three Rivers waiting for transportation to the Hurons, and there was Father Raymbault at Sainte Marie, his health ruined by a serious bout with pneumonia. He needed the care of the doctors at Quebec.

Isaac told Lalemant: "The trip absolutely must be made."

"Yes, but how?" asked Lalemant. "You cannot go all by yourself."

"Can't we make up a party from our own staff?"

It was worth discussing. A layman, Guillaume Couture, volunteered to make the trip; so did two others; a total of five men, and one of them, Raymbault, was too weak to be much help on the forty portages along the route.

The Hurons heard of the Jesuit plan. One day Eustace Ahatsistari, a great warrior of Teanaustayaé, came to the fort. He had been baptized the previous Holy Saturday. "You are seriously planning to make the trip?" he asked.

"We must, somehow," Lalemant said. "Suppose there is a sickness this winter, and we have no medicine? Suppose there is a drought this summer and nothing grows, and we have no food for the people? Suppose the Iroquois attack next winter and the people lose everything, and we have nothing to give them to wear or to hunt with or to build with? There is more danger in not making the trip, Eustace, than in making it."

"That is true," Eustace agreed, "and I have thought of that. I have talked to the Christian braves in my village and in Ossossané, and twenty of us have decided to escort the Blackrobes to Three Rivers if you really want to go. We know that it is for us that you must make the trip and so we feel we should share the danger with you."

Lalemant was so surprised, so touched, that for a moment he could not speak. Then he said: "This year, Eustace, the trip is not merely a trading expedition. It is a holy mission."

They chose Friday, June 13, as the departure day. On Thursday they packed four canoes with their travel equipment, with the Jesuit reports and with the few furs the people had collected during the winter. Early in the morning, Isaac and Charles Raymbault said their Masses; the French laymen and the Indians went to Confession and received Communion. Then with all others from the fort they went down to the river to the canoes, where everyone knelt for final prayers and blessings.

"God be with you, dear Isaac," Lalemant said as they moved down to the canoes.

"I know He will," Isaac said. "Whatever happens, we are ready for it."

"Be careful."

"Yes, of course." Isaac stepped gingerly into the lead canoe. He smiled broadly and waved as the canoe moved away from the beach. "Pray for us. We'll be back in two months."

But he was wrong. They would never be back.

CHAPTER SEVEN

1

THEY AGREED not to sacrifice safety for speed. Even here, so close to the fort, they held to the middle of the river, watching both banks, their paddle strokes cautious, steady. The inlet provided a measure of relief: wider than the river, it allowed time for retreat in case Iroquois canoes came dashing from the shore. Two hours later, they passed on their left the high bluff where Ihonatiria once stood, now a quiet and abandoned place. They chose a course more than a mile offshore, where the choppy waters of Georgian Bay impeded their progress even more, but they did not care. They could see clearly in all directions. They were alone.

Normally, the journey to the French River, in the northeast corner of the bay, required two days, perhaps two and a half; for the sake of caution, the flotilla took five days, camping at night on wide beaches where the trees were far back from the shoreline, and numerous guards were posted. To avoid detection, they went without fires, eating their corn mush cold. Mornings, they were up and on their way while the stars were still out.

The Nipissings were surprised to see them, particularly surprised to see so few of them. Leaders of the two tribes exchanged news, the Nipissings reporting that small bands of Iroquois had been seen nearby within the past few days. They were armed with muskets but had caused no trouble and were apparently on scouting assignments. The Hurons asked if the Nipissings would provide an escort across their country, but the Nipissings refused: in these dangerous times they did not choose to wander far from their village palisades.

The Christian caravan crossed the Lake of the Nipissings to the place where the long portage began to the Ottawa River. No sound could be trusted, no cry of a bird, no bark of a beast, no fall of a dead branch; everything had to be investigated. At last they arrived at the Ottawa, narrow and quiet at its source, with willows full and low along the banks, providing perfect ambushes for the Iroquois. Again the order went out: watch everything, hear everything, trust nothing. At portages along the way, a few men toted the cargo while the others lined the path, tomahawks in hand, arrows ready in the bow, eyes unblinking, ears alert, nostrils high to test the wind.

They reached the place of the Island Algonquins, pausing briefly to exchange news again. No Iroquois had been seen near the islands, but a report had come that they had sacked a village two days' walk to the south. Traditionally, the Hurons were forced to pay a tribute to the Algonquins at this point of their annual journey, but now when the subject arose the Algonquins said that this time no tribute was necessary: adversaries of both the Hurons and the Iroquois, the Algonquins did not want to be caught between them, and they urged the Hurons to pass quickly on their way.

With just four canoes, it was useless for the flotilla to send ahead an advance party. Strength lay in remaining close, presenting a fierce nub of resistance to any attack. At Eustace's suggestion, they traveled with the attitude that they were actually the attackers, seeking a good place to lurk in ambush. Thus they veered away from the mouths of creeks that bent quickly out of sight, from shorelines where the naked roots of big trees reached out into the water, from islands whose uninhabited appearance might be deceptive, and several times they risked violent rapids rather than take the portage paths which they knew from past trips led too deep into the dark forests.

They came to Montreal, where a mission station had been built on the big island, facing the Iroquois frontier on the southern banks of the St. Lawrence, just yards away. But the priests were not there. They had been recalled to Three Rivers earlier for their own safety and because they did not expect any Huron flotilla which they might join for the last leg of the trip.

Usually, covering the ninety miles from Montreal to Three Rivers by canoe required a night of camping out, but Eustace asked: "Why give them another chance to find us? We can continue traveling through the night, it will be safer."

"It will be a strain on the men, paddling so many hours," Isaac said.

"We can do it," Eustace assured.

They rested at Montreal until late at night, until they were confident that any Iroquois watching the important island had decided that no travelers would be leaving for down-river and had gone back to their camp. Clouds settled over the river; there was no moon. At two o'clock in the morning, the Huron party silently entered its canoes and started off, paddles cutting deep and steady and quietly into the still river. Even now they traveled cautiously, avoiding islands, rounding bends fully alert, sometimes choosing to make their way through swamps when they knew that the faster, open channel would take them too close to the southern banks.

Dawn came. The Iroquois would be stirring now, planning the day's attacks. Eustace led his men closer to the north shore. The morning hours continued to pass without a sign of the enemy. Where were they? Was it possible that the Iroquois preferred not to take any chances this near

Three Rivers, this near to the French soldiers stationed there? In the later afternoon, after fifteen hours of constant paddling, Eustace signaled them to head to the north shore.

He said to Isaac: "The river of the Iroquois is ahead and there are many islands. Let us rest here until night, when it will be safer to pass."

They went ashore and pulled their canoes into the woods after them, and they smoothed out the sand on the beach so that the Iroquois scouts would not be able to detect where they had landed. Again they did not build fires and they ate their food cold and they took turns sleeping. When at last it was late and quiet and dark they put their canoes back into the water and continued on their way.

They came to the islands and swung wide of them, then they passed the mouth of the river of the Iroquois, which the French called the Richelieu River, but they saw nothing, not even campfires. They entered the narrows that opened onto Lake St. Peter. Nothing. By dawn, they were almost across the lake, and they knew that the river beyond was wide: there would be less chance of an ambush. Much of the fear and worry went out of them: the worst was over. In an hour or two, they should begin to sing, as they normally did when they were this close to their destination, but they did not have the heart for it. They had made it, they had been lucky, they had been blessed, and for this they were quietly grateful, but the apprehensions with which they had lived for so long still clung to them, clung heavily because everybody knew they would have to go through it all again on the way home.

It was early morning when they landed on the beach at Three Rivers, and no one was about. Isaac Jogues noted that the journey had taken thirty-five days, almost twice the time of his own trip in the opposite direction six years before. From habit, he turned to help drag the canoes ashore and unpack them, but Eustace indicated that his men would do the work. An Algonquin woman stepped out of a tent, saw them and, startled by the sight of strangers, she screamed. Immediately Algonquin braves scrambled awake and grabbed their tomahawks and rushed out of their tents, expecting to see Iroquois, but when they saw the Blackrobes and recognized the hair style of the Hurons they were relieved and ran down to the beach, shouting greetings.

The whole settlement was quickly awake, full of wonder, full of questions, but for Isaac Jogues there were other matters of more importance. He led his Hurons to the Jesuit chapel and celebrated a Mass of Thanksgiving for them, then he took Communion to Father Raymbault, so seriously weakened by the arduous journey that he could not say a Mass.

Now there was time for talk. The Jesuits were amazed to hear Father Jogues's report, of his trip to the Ojibwas, of the severe winter at Sainte Marie, the dangers, the need for bastions and moats around a mission station, the Iroquois attacks. Convinced by Isaac that the Hurons would need another display of generosity to get through another winter, the traders agreed to pay as liberally as possible for the few furs that had been brought in. Meanwhile, Guillaume Couture began stockpiling the supplies to take back to Sainte Marie. At Quebec, Father Barthélemy Vimont had replaced Le Jeune as Superior of the New France missions, and it was necessary for Jogues to go to him to give an account of developments in the Huron country, to turn over reports and mail destined for France and to receive instructions for the coming winter.

Isaac had already learned that no new priests had arrived from France that spring. Vimont said: "And there will be none next year, I am informed."

"What about Father de Brébeuf?" Jogues asked. "Is he well enough to come back?"

"He is well enough, but I need him here."

That would cause disappointment at Sainte Marie, where the man was greatly admired and still regarded as a leader. Isaac said: "Well, we will just have to manage."

Father Vimont looked away. "As a matter of fact, since I learned that you were at Three Rivers, I have been thinking of keeping you here, too."

Isaac was stunned. "Father, let me go back!"

"We need every priest here we can get," said Vimont.

"But I am needed out there."

"You've been out there six years. It is time you had a rest, Father Jogues. The work here is easier and it is equally important."

"But what about the Hurons at Three Rivers?"

"They can take the mission supplies back to Father Lalemant whenever they are ready to leave," Vimont said.

Isaac Jogues shook his head. "I would not let them make so dangerous a journey without a priest."

Vimont studied Jogues for a moment, then said: "That is precisely what I thought you would say and it is the only one of your objections that I cannot bring myself to overrule. Very well, Father, you can return with the flotilla." Greatly relieved, Isaac sank back in his chair. Father Vimont went on: "Do you know René Goupil?"

"We met today."

In his youth, René Goupil had been a Jesuit seminarian,

but ill health forced him to abandon his studies and he subsequently went into medicine. Both his love of the Society
and his desire to be a missionary had persisted over the
years, and when the Jesuits announced in France that they
were willing to accept laymen to serve in Canada he was
among the first to come forward. Now, at thirty-four, Goupil had been at Quebec for three years. He was a small man,
but well-built and strong. His curly brown hair was beginning to recede, and he wore a neat brown beard. Happy to
be living the life which he had wanted since boyhood, he
always effused a warmth which instantly inspired warmth in
return.

Father Vimont said of him: "We are very fond of René.
He is a pious man, an inspiration. However, we have the
military doctors here, and the Ursuline Sisters who serve as
nurses as well as teachers. Now that Sainte Marie is growing so large, perhaps you can use René there?"

"We are in great need of a doctor," Jogues said.

"Tell that to René," Vimont suggested. "If he wants to go,
he may."

Goupil wanted very much to go. "You know, Father," he
confided to Jogues, "when I was a seminarian I felt I had a
vocation to work with the Hurons. Last year when I saw
them for the first time at Three Rivers, it was like meeting
long-lost relatives."

Jogues warned: "The trip will be dangerous."

"You are going," Goupil pointed out.

"It is my duty."

"It is mine, too."

They spent two days acquiring additional supplies, plus
the medical equipment Goupil would need. Goupil's delight
at being on his way made Isaac feel as though he were
Christmas shopping. At last, there was only one thing left
to do. At the Ursuline school was a thirteen-year-old girl,
Theresa, the daughter of Joseph Chihwatenhwa, who had

been a student with the Sisters for two years and was ready to go home now. Because of the dangers, Father Jogues suggested that she wait another year, but the girl said she was not afraid. "If I live and get home," she said, "I have learned much here I can use to help my mother, and if the Iroquois kill me on the way, as they killed my father, then I will join him in Heaven." This was one of the striking things about the Huron converts that deeply touched Isaac: man or woman or child, when they believed they believed fully, without question or hesitation, and they expected Heaven to be theirs just as confidently as they knew that one day death would be. The Blackrobes had taught them the Christian rules, they obeyed them, and they had no doubts about receiving the rewards. As presumptuous as this might be, it was nevertheless a proper confidence in good Christians, and Isaac welcomed it.

He welcomed, too, the other Hurons he met at Quebec who asked if they could make the trip home with him. They had spent the winter at Quebec, and now, because of the Iroquois, were prepared to spend another, but they had heard that Ondessonk was going to attempt the journey and they now wanted to try it, too. Eustace was glad to have the additional men along: the more men the less chance of attacks by small Iroquois bands. They left Quebec on Monday, July 28, and reached Three Rivers in two days. Here, too, were more Hurons eager to go home. Thus at dawn on Friday, August 1, when they all gathered at the beach for their departure prayers and farewells, there were twelve canoes in the flotilla, about fifty men and one girl.

That night they camped on the shores of Lake St. Peter, and they had a decision to make. The next day's travel would take them through the island section of the river. Should they swing south of the islands, into the open water, possibly in full view of any Iroquois who might be lurking on the southern banks of the river? Or should they proceed through the narrow passage north of the islands despite the risk of ambush it held? Isaac let Eustace decide. The narrow passage. True, it offered dangers, but it offered seclusion, too.

It was still dark when they ate their cold breakfast, just dawn when they moved out. An hour later, the islands were in sight. Eustace, in the lead canoe, guided his craft toward the narrows and the others followed. Another hour passed. The air was quiet here: there was no wind in the trees.

Then a brave saw something on the shore and shot his hand into the air. The line of canoes stopped. Eustace moved in for a look; two or three more canoes neared softly, Isaac in one of them. The men went ashore.

There were footprints in the mud, fresh footprints, and there were wedges made by canoes.

Isaac whispered: "Whose?"

"I don't know," Eustace replied. "I'm not sure."

A brave said: "Iroquois. Mohawks." The fiercest of the Iroquois tribes.

But another said: "The heel is not broad enough for Mohawks."

Eustace pointed to the wedges. "Three canoes. Fifteen, twenty men. We are more. They will not attack, whoever they are. Let us go on."

They slid their canoes back into the water. Eustace held up his tomahawk as a sign for the braves in the following canoes to be on the ready. René Goupil and Guillaume Couture examined their muskets to be sure they were loaded. Isaac, as a priest, was unarmed. He looked around to see if Theresa was all right and he saw that she was praying, and he added his own prayers to hers.

They moved on. Now the shoreline became a swamp and the wall of trees fell back some twenty yards. The broad space gave them a sense of safety. Up ahead, however, they could see the waiting danger, where the channel narrowed to a stream, and they watched it anxiously.

Then it came from across the swamp—the thunder of muskets. A delusion of safety had led the caravan directly into the line of fire. The five leading Huron canoes were trapped, but there was time for the rear seven to turn and escape. Isaac's canoe was hit and began to sink, and as the braves with him raced toward the bank he saw the other craft head in.

As the Hurons leaped ashore a short distance upstream from the swamp, they darted to high ground where they could observe the next move of the Mohawks. Father Jogues scrambled ashore, and in his rush to join the Hurons he tripped on slippery rocks, fell and rolled into a patch of tall grass. Lying there, he could clearly see ahead: the Hurons, Goupil among them, were crouched behind trees, watching the Mohawks come up from the swamp. To flee now was impossible; it was also unthinkable. Regardless of the odds, regardless of the superior Mohawk weapons, the Hurons were bound by their tribal values of pride and courage to stand their ground as long as they could. Jogues glanced about for Couture and Theresa, but he could not locate them. He saw the Mohawks, some forty of them, ascending the rise to the clear ground. The Mohawks outnumbered the Hurons two to one, but in close-in fighting the Mohawks would lose much of their supremacy because of the time needed to reload their muskets, and Jogues realized this was the moment the Hurons were awaiting.

It came. With a burst of war whoops, the Hurons rushed from their hiding places. From the Mohawks came a barrage—and then the Hurons were upon them. But in that same moment fresh battle cries came from the river as more Mohawks, fifty or sixty of them, slid their canoes ashore and raced up the hill. René Goupil fired into the crowd and downed a Mohawk, but before he could fire again three

Mohawks from the swamp pounced upon him and dragged him into the clearing. The Hurons fought bravely, their tomahawks and knives sinking into Mohawk flesh. Eustace battled like a wild man. Seven Mohawks had encircled him, lunging at him from all sides, beating him with their iron bars, sinking their teeth into his shoulders and legs. He swung at them, his hatchet grazing their skulls, his sharp knife slashing to the bone. Even when they finally succeeded in throwing him to the ground and piling on top of him, he bucked and squirmed, wrenching their weapons from their grasps. Goupil wriggled under the weight of five Mohawks who were pummeling him with their fists, crunching his fingers between their teeth, ripping his clothes off, pulling the beard hairs from his face. There was not a sound out of him.

Several Mohawks dashed into the woods, and in a few moments three of them returned with Theresa in front of them. They were prodding her, slapping her, knocking her down, and when they brought her into the clearing, where just two or three Hurons still resisted the Mohawks, they tied her up and threw her to the ground near Eustace.

It was then that one of the Mohawk braves recognized Eustace—Ahatsistari, the great Huron warrior! Quickly the news spread of the important capture the Mohawks had made. Two years before, Eustace, then a savage pagan, had led the Huron party which captured the Oneidas who had been burned to death and eaten at Teanaustayaé, and since then the entire Iroquois nation was sworn to revenge. Now the Mohawks had captured him. Triumphant, they broke out in dances, hopping first on one foot, then the other, and they sang out their joy in falsetto barks. Almost mischievously they assured each other that when they led Ahatsistari through the gates of their village there would be revenge indeed.

All the fighting was over now. From his hideout, Jogues

[115]

could see the Mohawks hoist their prisoners to their feet and shove them toward the water. As they prepared to move out, the Mohawk leaders quickly surveyed the battlefield: two Hurons were dead, one Mohawk, and several from both tribes sat on the ground attending their wounds and bruises. A few Mohawks were missing, but the leaders dismissed them with shrugs; if they were alive they could find their own way home.

Watching, Isaac Jogues assumed that the Mohawks believed he must have escaped, and in a way he had. As long as he remained motionless, the Mohawks could not see him, and it seemed that in a few minutes they would leave without searching for him. Also, it appeared that Couture had escaped; there had been no sign of him since the landing. Jogues, pondering his position, knew in his heart that his own escape, his own safety, was unimportant. Before his eyes, his friends, French and Huron, were being led away to certain death—death that would come mercifully after the great suffering of cruel torture. Father Jogues had witnessed such torture in the Huron villages and he knew what they could do to a man's spiritual stamina. There were Christians among the captured Hurons, and there was, of course, Goupil. Jogues realized he could not let them go through their torment without the consolation which he, as a priest, could provide, and he could not let the unbaptized Hurons face death without a chance for Heaven.

He got to his feet and walked the thirty yards out of the woods into the clearing and down toward the river. A Mohawk saw him, cried out, and all the others turned. Isaac Jogues raised his arms, both in blessing and in surrender. Several Mohawks approached cautiously, studying Jogues incredulously. A Blackrobe!

Jogues called out: "I am unarmed. I give myself to you." The Mohawks drew nearer, suspicious, the lances poised. "I am your prisoner," Jogues said.

The Mohawks flew at him, knocked him to the ground and began to beat him. They tore off his soutane and tossed it to each other, like boys with a ball. If capturing Eustace had been a cause for joy, capturing the French Blackrobe was a cause for ecstasy, and again there was singing and shouting. Other Mohawks, meanwhile had located the Huron canoes and dug into the cargo—axes, cloth, nails, dried fruit, wampum. There was a keg of Mass wine; the Mohawks opened it and sampled it. Firewater. To be sure, it was a great day.

In their excited celebrations, the Mohawks ignored their prisoners. With effort and pain, Isaac Jogues got to his feet and made his way to Eustace. Blood streamed down the Huron's face and from the wounds where the Mohawks had bitten him, but he gave no sign of pain: it would have been beneath his dignity as a great warrior to let the Mohawks know that their torture had caused him the slightest discomfort. The priest made the sign of the cross over Eustace, then touched his arm consolingly.

"Ondessonk, why did you show yourself?" Eustace asked. "You could have been free."

"My place is with you."

"It will be bad for us, Ondessonk."

"I know." Jogues turned to Theresa and he blessed her. "Are you all right, my dear?"

She nodded once, her eyes full of fear. "Will they make me a slave, do you think, Father?" she asked.

"I don't know," Jogues said. "We are in God's hands; He will protect all of us." He moved on to Goupil, who lay alone several feet away. The Frenchman's eyes were blackened, several of his teeth were missing, some of his fingernails had been ripped off by Mohawk teeth, his face bled where patches of beard had been pulled out. In silence, the two men examined each other's bruised face;

then Isaac said: "God asks strange things of us sometimes, René."

"I accept whatever He asks," said Goupil. Then: "Father, I want to confess."

Father Jogues moved close and listened. A few moments later, while he was holding up his hand in absolution, a shot came from the woods—then another. The celebrating Mohawks stopped in their tracks and stared in astonishment. Then five of them, recovering from the surprise, picked up their muskets and hurried into the woods, their squat, solid bodies light upon their quick, tense step, their deep voices soft barks of warning. In the clearing, all was still for several minutes until the Mohawks came back into sight. Two of them were carrying the dead body of another Mohawk, while the remaining three goaded ahead of them the missing Guillaume Couture. His arms were bound behind him and he had been beaten. He stumbled to the other prisoners and dropped to his knees.

Jogues went to him. "I thought you had escaped."

"I did," said Couture, "but I decided to come back. In the woods, this one"—he indicated the dead Mohawk—"and I saw each other at the same time, but I fired first."

"But why did you decide to come back?" Jogues asked, almost angry. Before answering, Couture looked from Jogues to Goupil, to Eustace and Theresa, to the other prisoners, and Jogues recognized on the young man's face the same concern he had felt while he was safe in his hideout, then Couture said evasively: "I was lonely."

Isaac understood. "Lonely for Heaven," he said.

The Mohawks were ready now. They gathered their prisoners together, twenty-three of them, including the Frenchmen and the girl. Two Hurons had been killed, two Mohawks, one by Couture, but many on both sides had been injured. The dead were left behind when the Mohawks and their prisoners boarded the canoes and began to move downstream. And all the prisoners knew that they would have been better off if they, too, had been left behind, dead upon a clearing in the wilderness.

3

That night they camped at the mouth of the river of the Iroquois, on the plateau where the French were planning to build a fort which, they hoped, would serve to keep the Iroquois canoes out of the St. Lawrence. In the morning they arose early to begin the long journey to the Mohawk villages, far to the south. The prisoners were given no peace. At rest stops—to eat or to sleep or for a portage, the Mohawks assaulted the prisoners anew. Scabs formed on the prisoners' wounds and the Mohawks scraped them off. When too much blood seemed to flow, the Mohawks stopped the stream by applying red-hot irons. Only Theresa went untouched, as though she were being saved for something special.

The French got the worst of it since they, under Champlain, had helped the Algonquins defeat the Mohawks in battle, and now the Mohawks had their opportunity for a long-awaited revenge. As for Isaac Jogues, he was a Blackrobe, and the Blackrobes had befriended the Hurons, which made the priest a double enemy, the double victim of their tortures.

Three young Mohawk braves, hardly more than boys, were Isaac's chief tormentors. Every chance they had, they beat him and badgered him, pounding him with hot pokers, bursting open his wounds, and they chewed on his fingers until they were pulp. Usually Isaac and Goupil rode in the same canoe, and Goupil tried to comfort Isaac by making bandages out of scraps of his shirt and his leggings.

The prisoners could not sleep at night; their bodies were too severely gashed with festering sores. Flies and mosquitoes crawled over them; maggots appeared in their wounds. So they lay awake, and those who could not lie down knelt or stood or tried to brace themselves against trees, while Isaac spoke to them softly about God; or they said the rosary or Theresa sang the French hymns she had learned at school. Sometimes, if they were fortunate, the excruciating weight of their suffering pulled them briefly but mercifully down into unconsciousness and their torn muscles were able to relax briefly until the Mohawks aroused them for another brutal day.

The deeper they penetrated into Mohawk country the more scouting parties they encountered, and each encounter meant another victory celebration, which meant another beating. On the fifth day, they entered Lake Champlain and they made their way to a large island where two hundred Mohawks were encamped. Again they heard the cries of wonder: Hurons! Tremendous booty! Ahatsistari! Frenchmen! A Blackrobe! The Mohawks scattered, then were back in a few moments, armed with clubs, irons, chains, and firebrands, and they formed a double line down a hillside.

Couture recognized what was about to happen. "The gauntlet."

The prisoners were lined up—first Couture, then some Hurons, then Theresa, then Hurons, then Goupil, more Hurons, then Eustace, the remaining Hurons, then Isaac. Mohawk guards began to beat them, urging them to run, and they ran where they were led, to the double row of Mohawks lining the hill. One by one, they were forced to dash up the hill between the rows of howling Mohawks, and at each step they were beaten and branded and burned. By the time Goupil made the dash, the Mohawks were in a frenzy; by the time Eustace ran the gauntlet, the Mohawks were foaming in perverse ecstasy, and when it was Isaac's turn they had reached their pitch. He slipped in the mud, on blood-wet grass, falling, sliding, groveling. Purposely each pair of Mohawks pounded at his legs so he would fall in front of them and they would have him to themselves longer. His shirt caught fire; the stench of his singed beard sickened him. An eternity later he fell into Goupil's arms. Goupil dragged him aside and gently patted out the flames and held him in his arms and cooled his face with tears.

But it was not over. The Mohawks built a big fire and when it was roaring high they corralled the prisoners around it and shouted: "Dance! Dance! Sing! Let's see you dance! Let's hear you sing!" And when the prisoners were too weak to move, barely able to stand, the Mohawks swept thick burning faggots across the prisoners' legs and there was nothing to do but dance. In the Indian fashion, they stamped first on one foot and then on the other, their arms raised, swaying, turning, bobbing; and because they were ordered to sing, they moaned and whined a meaningless chant. The Frenchmen did not look at each other in order to preserve each other's last shreds of decency in this barbaric humiliation.

In the morning they were on the move again, southward, requiring two more days to reach the end of the lake. Here the Mohawks left their canoes, indicating that the rest of the journey would be made by foot. Fortunately, Isaac had retrieved his shoes from the Huron canoe on the day of the ambush, or else, he knew, he would not be able to take a step. Even so, his feet were all blisters and each step was great pain. He was forced to walk slowly, dropping to the end of the line. Goupil lagged behind to accompany him.

One day, Goupil said: "Father, do you know that I was studying for the Society?"

"Yes."

"I had to give it up. Tuberculosis. My heart broke when I left school."

"I'm sure."

"More than anything, more than ever now, I wish that I could die a Jesuit."

"I am happy that I shall."

They walked along. Goupil tested: "Father, do you think this may be one of those emergencies they're always mentioning in canon law, when a priest is free to do whatever he feels he must?"

"What do you mean?" Isaac asked.

"We are near death, Father. I want to die a Jesuit. I want to take my vows. Will you let me pronounce them to you?"

They stopped and faced each other. Emergency? Would they ever face one more critical? Whatever canon law might say, this was an emergency. The request was literally a dying man's last wish. Isaac said: "Yes, of course, René."

They put down the bundles the Mohawks made them carry and they knelt while René Goupil whispered the words he had memorized years ago, when, as a seminarian, his only wish was that one day he might kneel in a sanctuary and recite them to the Jesuit authorities. He offered his life in obedience to the Jesuit rule, pledging to live thereafter in poverty and chastity, as indeed he had thus far, and asking of God: ". . . I most humbly beseech Thee, by Thy Infinite Goodness and Mercy, that Thou wilt vouchsafe to admit this holocaust in an odor of sweetness and that as Thou hast already given me grace to desire and offer it so Thou wilt bestow plentiful grace on me to fulfill it. Amen."

Isaac said: "Amen." He blessed Goupil, and they remained kneeling in thankfulness that this occasion had been afforded them. A Mohawk up ahead called to them to hurry along. Isaac said: "Come, Brother René."

The Mohawk food was running low. The unexpected capture of over twenty prisoners, who had to be fed, drained the supply of crushed corn faster than the Mohawks had anticipated. By the eighth day, there was no corn left at all. In less pressing circumstances the Mohawks might have stopped to fish or hunt, but they were still exhilarated over their success, impatient to get home and display their spoils. Moreover, for the Mohawks—and for the Hurons, too, for that matter, and under normal conditions—a day or two, even three, without food was no great ordeal; they were raised for hardship. But for the prisoners, particularly the French, the lack of food compounded the miseries of weakness from the loss of blood, torment from infected wounds, anguish from pulverized bones and rent muscles. The caravan slowed down. Not all the threats and proddings and lashes of the Mohawks could make the prisoners step along.

Invariably, Jogues and Goupil brought up the rear. When Jogues knew how far behind they were, he repeatedly urged Goupil: "Escape. Go. The Mohawks will not miss you until night. Head straight north to the St. Lawrence. Go, René."

Always Goupil said: "No, I will stay with you."

So they often dragged into camp hours after the others, dropping in their tracks and praying for sleep. And in the morning, to get the energy to stand, they chewed mouthfuls of wet grass.

Then, one night, when the two Jesuits at last staggered into camp, they saw women and children and more men than before, and they could smell food cooking in the pots nestled in the fire. Isaac and René ran forward to the fires and reached for the pots, but the Mohawks caught them, laughed and shoved them aside. They tumbled to where the other prisoners lay waiting for food.

[123]

Isaac found himself near Eustace. "What is it, Eustace? What's happening?"

"The war party sent scouts ahead to have food brought out from the village."

"Are we near a village?"

"We will be at Ossernenon tomorrow," Eustace said.

"Tomorrow." Perhaps their last day on earth.

"There will be many Mohawks, Ondessonk. The word has spread about us, and the people are coming from other villages. It will be bad."

Isaac nodded, resigned. Could it be any worse?

The newcomers browsed among the prisoners, rolling them over for a look at their faces, jeering at them, snapping birch whips at their bare flesh. Jogues and Eustace were the prize displays, now conveniently side by side. The crowd gathered around, pointing, laughing. A boy dashed in and sprinkled glowing ashes in Isaac's face and on Eustace's naked chest. Two braves of the war party brought pots of corn mush and placed them just beyond reach of the prisoners. The famished French and Hurons scurried forward to the pots, digging into them with their hands, and the sight of the starving prisoners scrambling for food struck the Mohawks as great comedy.

The triumphant Mohawks caroused all night. They made a game of seeing who could get closest to the prisoners with a white-hot poker without being detected. Because Father Jogues was the prize prisoner, it was he they taunted most.

At dawn, the prisoners were aroused and given another meal. Their last? The Mohawks were busily breaking camp, eager to be on their way on the few remaining miles to Ossernenon. At a good pace, they could reach home in five hours. The line was formed, the march begun, and this time there would be no laggards. The Mohawks who had joined the party the night before now paraded alongside the prisoners and were quick to whip any who hesitated, even for the necessary moment to adjust their bundles. Each hour added more Mohawks to the raucous victory procession. Songs broke out, one chant crashing against another in frenzied cacophony. Warriors who had taken part in the ambush skipped and pranced and bucked and lunged, demonstrating how brave they had been in the fight.

The Hurons would not be outdone. They too had been brave, they too had fought well, and they had lost merely because they were outnumbered by enemies armed with muskets, so despite their battered bodies they puffed up their chests and threw back their heads, putting hatred and disgust on their faces as they sang their own songs in lusty defiance, keeping up the trot demanded of them as though the agonies of the past two weeks had never occurred.

The French were incapable of such resilience. They stumbled and tripped along, eyes glazed by exhaustion, open mouths gasping for air. They dropped their bundles, then quickly scooped them up and dodged the Mohawk whips. Isaac's body was wet with blood from his agitated wounds, Goupil swung his bundle to his shoulders to ward off the Mohawk blows, Couture lumbered blindly onward.

They came to the muddy, sluggish, winding Mohawk River, about eighty feet wide at this point. Beyond, a steep hill rose to a plateau, and they saw the palisade of Ossernenon. The river was thick with Mohawk canoes: they could have walked across. Up the hill and across the plateau, a sea of Mohawks stormed in wild hunger. At the sight of the prisoners, a roar went up that shook the trees.

Isaac Jogues looked out at the tempest of clubs, whips, chains, hammers, paddles and iron rods. My God.
My God.

CHAPTER EIGHT

1

Isaac Jogues wondered why God was keeping them alive. They had all suffered so much. They were willing to suffer more, if that was what God wanted; but since they had already suffered enough to kill any man, they could not understand why they were not dead. Their journey from Sainte Marie had been a religious expedition: of this they had no doubt. In order that the mission might have supplies and equipment to help the starving Hurons through the winter, they had, in the name of Christian charity, made the dangerous voyage, and they felt that everything that had happened to them since the ambush was an outgrowth of their decision to act as Christians. The same was true of those like Goupil and Theresa, who had joined the flotilla at Quebec with Christian intentions. This was no deluded effort to enshroud their coming deaths with holy martyrdom. To the prisoners, it was plain fact, and it was this conviction alone that enabled them to retain their sanity. Although they were willing to suffer anything and to suffer any amount because of God, for God and in His Name, they could not understand how mere human beings could survive so much—and for so long.

The Ossernenon gauntlet was a barbaric example. Hundreds of Mohawks long, it stretched up the hill and down, then up again, across the plateau and around the village, forever, forever. Only Theresa was saved from the full length

of it. After her first few steps she fell to the ground uncon-
scious and the Mohawks kicked her aside. But the men took
the full hell of it, and the Frenchmen took the fullest. They
were almost torn to shreds. At the end, they lay in a battered
heap near the gate of the village. The Hurons seemed im-
pervious to their pains; those who could see stared blankly
at the sky. Even now they would not give the Mohawks the
satisfaction of knowing they had inflicted the slightest pain.
If the French did not seem agonized, it was simply because
they could not move their muscles to display it. Goupil's
beaten face, Jogues observed, made him look like a leper.
Couture lay in such distorted positions that Isaac was convinced the man did not have an unbroken bone in his body.
Father Jogues's own anguish throbbed anew in him with
each heartbeat. The noon sun burned down on all of them.
Goupil was protected from the scorching rays only by the
tattered shirt he wore. All that was left of Isaac's clothes
were his leggings, shoes, and torn pants. Couture had nothing on.

Suddenly the peace of undisturbed suffering was broken
by the approach of the Mohawks. The three Frenchmen
were lifted from the ground and hoisted to the five-foot
platform which stood at the entrance to the village, and
the crowd gathered around.

A chief bounded up on the platform, an iron rod in his
hand. He began to rant about what a great day this was
for the Mohawks, how proud everyone should be of the
braves who had captured the Frenchmen, what a victory
feast was ahead after the French had been roasted over a
fire. Then he struck each one of them on the back with
his poker, three times. Jogues slithered from the stage and
fell to the ground. The crowd howled with laughter.

An Algonquin woman, a slave, was brought forward, and
a knife was handed to her. The chief called down: "Cut off

his thumb." The woman hesitated, studying Isaac fearfully. The chief called again: "Cut off his thumb!"

The woman stepped near and, to Isaac's surprise, whispered in French: "I am a Christian, Father. I was baptized at Three Rivers. I cannot do this to you."

The chief called: "Cut off his thumb or I will cut off yours!"

Jogues held out his left hand and extended his thumb and steadied it with his right hand. "Do what you must do."

The woman put the sharp blade at the base of Isaac's left hand and made several small cuts to find the joint. Finding it, she cut deep, bending the thumb back to expose the tendons, and she slashed through them, twisting the thumb to break the tissue that held it in its socket. The thumb came off. Isaac took the thumb in both hands and held it high in his palms as often in the past he had held high the Host on a paten, and he offered this severed part of himself to God.

He heard Eustace urge: "Throw it away, Ondessonk, throw it away or they will make you eat it."

He threw the thumb away and the children scrambled for it.

On the stage, the chief pounced on Goupil and, holding the Frenchman's right hand in the air, slashed off the first joint of the thumb and threw it to the children. And all the Mohawks began to howl and dance and sing.

In the afternoon, the prisoners were taken to a cabin and given something to eat. Then the last of their clothes were taken from them. They were forced to lie on their backs, tied at the wrists and ankles to stakes hammered into the ground, and they were left there for the night. Ants and fleas crawled into their wounds; the air stank from their own rotting flesh. From Jogues and Goupil rose the odor of burnt meat, where hot pokers had been applied to their hands to stop the bleeding. From time to time, children came in to sprinkle sizzling coals on the prisoners and to watch them squirm helplessly. The Mohawk children, not used to seeing beards on men, pulled out the face hairs of the Frenchmen to find out if they were real.

Next morning, after they had been untied and given a meal, they learned they were to be taken on a tour of neighboring Mohawk villages, to be shown off and to be submitted to the tortures of people who had not been able to get to Ossernenon. The Mohawks came for them at noon, and as they stepped out of the cabin to the waiting crowd Isaac became acutely aware of his nudity. He asked a Mohawk brave: "Can't I be given something to wear?"

"What for?" the brave asked.

How could the priest explain Christian modesty? He did not try. He pointed at the sky. "The sun is very hot." The brave gave him a square of cloth, too small for the purpose he desired. He put it around his neck, but it was rough cloth that cut into his sensitive sores. He gave it back.

The village of Andagaron was six miles away. Long before the procession of Mohawks and prisoners reached the last turn on the path that opened onto the village, they could hear the Andagaron drums and chants, and when the village came into view they saw the excited people already lined up for the gauntlet. To one side was the now familiar stage on which they were to be mocked and tortured. The torment lasted all afternoon. When they were on the platform, an Andagaron brave, noticing that Guillaume Couture still had two undamaged fingers, climbed to the stage, a shell clenched between his teeth, and when he discovered that the shell would not cut through the bone he merely twisted and bent and pulled on each finger until it came off. Couture's arm expanded like a balloon and he fainted. The Mohawks thought he had died and they carried him away, but somehow he survived.

[129]

That night the prisoners were again tied to the ground in a cabin and again subjected to the perverse games of the children. Morning brought a sky black with storm. Nevertheless, the prisoners were taken back to the platform, but before the day's fury could begin the storm broke, sending down a violence of rain, thunder and lightning. The Mohawks returned to their cabins, leaving the prisoners on the platform. All day the French and Hurons remained there, cold, wet, miserable. This was the first chance they had to be together in any semblance of peace, and Father Jogues used the occasion to hear confessions, to encourage and comfort spiritually, to remind all of them that their suffering would be meaningless unless they offered it up to Jesus Christ as penance for their sins and in recognition of what He had suffered at Calvary for them.

The rain stopped with evening. The Mohawks, made lazy by their inactive day, were content to gather around the stage and taunt the prisoners into dancing for them, inspiring them by throwing flaming branches at their feet. Compared to the usual Mohawk extremes, this torture was merciful.

2

They went next to Tionontoguen, to another gauntlet, to another stage. By now, Isaac Jogues had lost not only his left thumb but the first two joints on his right index and little fingers. Each morning, his hands were thick with black pus. At Tionontoguen, Eustace lost both his thumbs, the most degrading punishment that could be inflicted upon him: if he lived, he would no longer be able to brace a bow in his hands to send an arrow against an enemy: his warrior days were over. But then he did not expect to live.

The Tionontoguen braves concocted a special humiliation

for Jogues. One evening, when the prisoners were taken to a cabin, the braves hoisted Isaac to a crossbeam, slung his arms over it, then tied his wrists to his upper arms. As he hung there, they used him for a swing, gripping his legs to ride back and forth. They also used him for a target, throwing garbage and mud at him. After more than an hour of this, a brave from another village came in, disliked what he saw and cut Isaac's ropes. He dropped to the ground, a heap of anguish, and remained there the whole night.

The Mohawk chiefs and sachems agreed that a decision must soon be made about the prisoners, which were to die, which were to become slaves, but first a few more villages awaited the prisoners. After this, the Mohawk leaders planned a council to be held at Andagaron. The people were growing impatient, eager to feast on the Huron and French flesh. It was expected that the prisoners would be divided up among the leading villages proportionately. The night before the prisoners left Tionontoguen, however, four new Huron captives were brought in, and the chiefs decided that two of them would be eaten immediately. Isaac Jogues knew the four men; they were astonished to see him; news of his capture had not as yet reached Sainte Marie. Isaac also knew the men were not baptized. He went to the two marked for immediate death and told them the things about God which they had heard him relate back in their villages. Fully aware that they were soon to die, they asked him to baptize them. Later, Jogues stood near the fires and prayed with the two men as they died. The other two, the chiefs decided, would be put to the fires on the night of the council at Andagaron. On the march to the village the prisoners had to ford a waist-deep stream, and it was here that Isaac was able to baptize the remaining two victims.

The council was held after the feast. The taste of Hurons still fresh in their mouths, the chiefs looked forward to allocating the remaining twenty Huron prisoners. The most important chiefs and sachems lived at Tionontoguen, so it was agreed that they should get the prize Huron: Eustace. His nephew, Paul, was consigned to Ossernenon, and the strong warrior Stephen went to Andagaron. The girl Theresa was also considered a prize, and for this reason she, too, was committed to Tionontoguen. The allocation of the seventeen braves, based on their age and physique, was easily and quickly resolved. As for the Frenchmen, one of them— Couture—had killed a Mohawk warrior during the ambush battle; tribal custom required that he be given to the family of the dead brave, to be killed, if they wished, or held in slavery, and the family lived in Tionontoguen. Finally, since most of the braves in the ambush party were from Ossernenon, the remaining Frenchmen—Jogues and Goupil—were to be allotted to that village as a reward. The idea was proposed of holding these two for a high ransom the French at Quebec might readily pay, but it was sternly rejected by the Ossernenon chiefs. Their village had suffered most in the fight against Champlain and the Algonquins; it was their privilege to deal with the two prisoners as they saw fit. The other chiefs conceded, but they pointed out that when news of the ambush reached Quebec the French might start a war in order to rescue their countrymen. Until this eventuality was determined, the chiefs urged, the Ossernenon leaders should not be too hasty in killing two prisoners who could subsequently prove to be valuable hostages. The precaution was accepted reluctantly.

So the moment came for the prisoners to say good-by to each other. "Be strong in your faith," Father Jogues advised them. "Trust always in God, for He will be with you at the end, waiting for you to go to Him. Keep your hearts free of hate against your tormentors. Forgive them, whatever they do, as Jesus forgave." To those bound for Tionontoguen he instructed that special care should be taken of Theresa so that, dead or alive, she could leave the Mohawk country as pure as she had entered it. He blessed them all, gave them absolution, and they said good-by.

That night they were all in their assigned villages, and that night Eustace and Paul and Stephen were killed and eaten.

Isaac Jogues and René Goupil were prepared to be thrust to the same death at any hour, but one day emptied into another and nothing happened. Their wounds and festering sores began to heal. Although they were still kicked, beaten and taunted, the punishments were sporadic and usually occurred only when they made the mistake of passing too near a Mohawk in an ill mood. The man who headed the cabin where they lived clearly disliked them and saw to it that they did not get enough to eat and that they did all chores that came along but the man could not evict them or kill them because of the responsibility for them he had been given. As slaves, they were rated lower than women. They had to go to the fields with the women, take orders there from the women, and if any woman felt like venting her temper on them she was free to do so.

They were given some cast-off clothes, tattered shirts and pants made of deerskin, and a brave gave them moccasins he had almost worn through. The booty taken at the ambush was carefully examined and distributed, but the two prisoners received none of it. However, there had been reading matter in the supply bundles; the Mohawks saw no harm in letting Jogues have a pamphlet edition of the *Epistle of St. Paul to the Hebrews*, which proved to be a source of great spiritual consolation for him and Goupil. At Tionontoguen, Couture was having an easier time. Although he was kept busy at hard work, the dead brave's family was tolerant with him, and he was granted permission to visit Isaac at Ossernenon. He was thus able to go to confession and to bring news of the other Christians at Tionontoguen. One day, some Ossernenon braves had to go to Tionontoguen

[133]

and they took Isaac along to carry their bundles. The occasion enabled Isaac to hear the confessions of all the Christians there and to spend a few hours encouraging them. Slave life, then, though certainly not a happy existence, was nonetheless better than their first weeks as prisoners had been. They were alive, at least. Some of them dared hope they might one day be free.

News of the French prisoners reached Rensselaerswyck, the Dutch settlement forty miles away on the site of what eventually became Albany, New York. Arendt Van Corlaer, director of the colony, was amazed, and he rushed word down the Hudson River to his superiors at Fort Amsterdam. The Mohawk-Dutch alliance was a fragile thing which the Dutch knew the Mohawks would break whenever it suited their purposes. Actually, the Dutch had no love for the French, either in the New World or the Old, and it had been in the hope of strengthening their own position with the Indians that they equipped the Iroquois with muskets and had propagandized against the French people and the French religion. But now circumstances were changed. Whatever else they were, the prisoners were Europeans. Orders came from New Amsterdam for Van Corlaer to take any necessary steps short of actual war to free them.

He set out for the Mohawk villages immediately. At Ossernenon, he had no luck at all. At his request, a high-level council was called at Tionontoguen, but he still made no headway. The Mohawk leaders told him that, regardless of their friendship, the French prisoners were no business of the Dutch. Van Corlaer turned to avenues he thought the Mohawks might readily travel: he offered to buy freedom for the Frenchmen, and at a price greater than the Mohawks could hope to earn from five years of trading furs. But they refused.

An important chief said: "You do not understand our purpose. We intend to take the Frenchmen back to Three

Rivers and use their freedom as a means of making a peace treaty with their country."

Later, Goupil asked Jogues: "Do you believe that?"

"No," Isaac said. "It was their way of putting the Dutch off. I wonder if the Dutchman believed it?"

Van Corlaer did not know what to believe. He reported his failure to New Amsterdam, assuring that he would try again and again. The next ship for Holland carried news of the prisoners to all Europe. Through Algonquin tribes living along the East Coast, the news traveled by couriers north to Quebec and Three Rivers.

Jogues and Goupil returned to their work and their prayers. In order to submerse himself wholly in his private spiritual exercises, Isaac sometimes went alone to some unfrequented place in the woods, where he would scratch a cross on a tree with a sharp stone and kneel before it, thus directing his thoughts more specifically to the symbol for which he lived, for which he suffered and for which he knew he would die. Another reason he sought the privacy was his realization of how much the Mohawks loathed such overt displays of Christian piety. Goupil was aware of this hatred, but he was inclined to be incautious about it. Wherever he might be, in the cabin, along the village paths, out in the fields, when he felt moved to pray, he knelt, made the sign of the cross upon himself, and said his prayers aloud, his heart sometimes moved to heavy sighs, occasionally to tears. When the Mohawks saw him at it, they struck him with their war clubs and sent him sprawling.

"You ought to be careful," Isaac told him. "Say your prayers privately. Pray you must, of course, but for your own sake don't antagonize the Mohawks with it."

In the cabin where they lived was a baby, and Goupil was fond of it. On rainy days or in the hours when there was no work, he would play with the boy. The Mohawks in the cabin gave no sign of how they felt about this. One after-

noon when he had the infant in his arms Goupil did what
for him was a natural expression of affection for a man like
himself: he took the baby's right hand and guided it in making the sign of the cross.

The headman of the cabin saw this and, infuriated, he
snatched the boy out of Goupil's arms and ordered the
Frenchman out of the house.

Goupil left the long house, and he decided it might be
wise if he left the village for a while, too. He was on the
path toward the woods when he saw Jogues returning from
his prayers.

Isaac perceived something was wrong. "What is it, René?
What's happened?" Goupil told him and Isaac said sadly:
"Oh, René, what an unfortunate mistake."

"I know, Father," Goupil said. "I didn't think. It was such
a natural thing to do with a baby; I've done it so often before."

"But not with a Mohawk baby."

"No."

Jogues looked ahead at the village. "Maybe we should
stay out for a while. Come, let's walk. We can say a rosary."

They turned and walked away from the village and began to say the rosary. They had said four decades when
they saw two braves step from the trees and block their
path. It was late September, the air was crisp; the braves
wore blankets. The two Jesuits immediately detected trouble, but they knew that if they tried to avoid the braves
they would surely get it.

"Pray to yourself," Isaac said, "and if anything happens
remember to call upon the Lord."

They continued the slow, casual walk, approaching,
reaching them, then passing them. Isaac took a few more
steps, then he heard: "Jesus, Jesus, Jesus!" He turned.

One brave had grabbed Goupil by the shoulders and
forced him to his knees. The other whipped a tomahawk

[136]

from under his blanket, swung it into the air, then sank the blade into Goupil's skull.

"Dear Lord!" Isaac gasped.

Goupil managed: "Jesus . . ."

The tomahawk whistled through the air again and cracked Goupil's skull. The brave holding Goupil released his grasp. Goupil fell over dead. Isaac stepped to him, knelt, and said the words of absolution and the prayers for the dying. His friend was gone.

He looked up at the braves, the question *why* in his eyes.

"He made the evil sign in the cabin," one brave said.

Still kneeling, Father Jogues made the sign of the cross upon himself, for he was sure it now was his turn. But the second brave said: "Go back to the village, to your cabin." Isaac began to gather Goupil in his arms. "Go back," the brave ordered.

"I must bury him," Jogues said.

"Leave him where he is," the brave demanded. He raised his tomahawk. "Go back."

The priest arose and obeyed.

The evening meal was in the pot when Isaac entered the cabin and the place where he always sat to eat was vacant for him. Custom required him to sit, but he could not bring himself to eat and did not reach into the pot. He stared at the fire, letting his tears flow down his cheeks.

The old man who, Jogues knew, had given the order to kill Goupil studied him for a moment, then spat the word: "Woman!"

Hours later, when all the others were asleep, Isaac got up, left the cabin and went out to the place where Goupil had been murdered, and he looked for his friend's body, but he could not find it. The spot where Goupil had fallen was still wet with blood. Isaac put his hand to it and then kissed the moistness of his palm, for he was convinced this blood was now a holy substance. He prayed for his friend; he prayed

[137]

to him, and addressed him as Saint René, truly believing him
to be precisely that—not only because of the way he had
died but because of the way he had lived.

3

All the next day, Isaac Jogues could not find Goupil's body.
A woman told him the braves had thrown it into the river.
A man said the braves had taken it deep into the woods
and left it there for the wolves to eat. A boy said he had
seen children playing with it: they had tied a rope around
it and made a game dragging it around; when they had
wearied of the game they threw the body in the ravine, a
half-mile southwest of the village where the women dumped
their garbage. Isaac knew the ravine. Its sides were steep,
its floor covered perhaps two acres, and a narrow, rapid
creek ran through it, emptying into the nearby Mohawk. He
went to the ravine and he dug through the garbage that
had piled up over the years, until he found Goupil, part of
his body already devoured by dogs and rats.

Reverently, he drew the body aside and brushed it clean.
He said more prayers. Now, where to bury Goupil? Isaac
had left his work without permission; he would soon be
missed; he had to get back. He decided on a temporary
burial until he had more time. The only safe place he could
see was in the creek. Lowering Goupil's body into the water,
he covered it with rocks until it could not be seen from the
banks and would not float away.

He went back to work. Later, when it was time to go into
the village, he saw an old woman standing at his cabin.
He knew her: the daughter of a chief, she had been the
squaw of a chief and the mother of chiefs. Thus she was one
of the few respected women in the village; she had even
been allowed to sit in on councils.

"Nephew," she said to him as he approached, and by this greeting he was aware of her concern for him. "Nephew, this long house is not a place for you any more. I have talked to the great chief. You are in my charge now and you will live in my house."

"Yes, Aunt."

"Do you have any belongings in here?" She indicated the cabin.

"I have nothing."

"Then go to my cabin. The pot is on the fire."

After the meal was over and the village went quiet, Isaac got up and made for the door. Aunt said: "Don't go out."

"I must do something, Aunt."

"Don't go out."

"This thing is important."

"I don't care what it is. I tell you don't go out."

"Why, Aunt?"

She said nothing, but her persistence convinced him that she knew of some danger that awaited him outside, so he went back to the fire, sitting there in silence until the hour came for sleep. From his habit in the former cabin, Jogues withdrew to a place far from the fire.

Aunt asked: "What are you doing over there?"

"Is this not the place for a slave?" he asked.

She pointed to a spot near her. "This is your place."

A deerskin lay there, a comfort he had not had since his capture. Aunt got up and fetched a blanket from the shelf and gave it to him, the first kind gesture shown him in almost two months. Aunt stood over him, looking down at him for a moment, then she went back to a dark corner of the cabin, and when she returned Isaac saw that she had a small object in her hands. As she neared, he recognized it as a book. She gave it to him. It was the *Imitation of Christ*, his copy, which he had last seen when he packed it at Quebec.

He was overjoyed. "Oh, Aunt, I thank you for this! Where did you get it?"

She had no intention of telling him. Whatever she felt toward him, she was a Mohawk, and she believed that the less she told anybody the better off she was. She rolled over and went to sleep. Isaac Jogues read until the embers in the fire were too dim for him to see by.

Aunt kept Isaac busy in the cabin for three or four days. He had scarcely a moment outside, but he knew that Aunt had her reasons for keeping him imprisoned. Finally, when she was apparently confident that the danger was over, the Mohawk braves now occupied with something else, she took him out to the field to help harvest what few vegetables remained in her patch. Isaac observed that the old woman intentionally turned her back on him for long periods of time, as though she did not want to see what he might do. When he was sure none of the other women were watching him, he moved quickly from the field and hurried to the ravine to recover Goupil's body and bury it properly.

He knew exactly where he had hidden it, but when he reached the creek he could not find the mounds of rocks. He glanced around to get his bearings, assured that this was the precise place. But there was no mound. Allowing that he might be wrong, he walked the full length of the bank, studying each foot of the creek bed. He saw nothing. He waded into the creek, now chest-deep from a rain, and with his feet he examined the entire bed as it coursed through the ravine. Nothing.

Grief-stricken, he could only deduce that someone had watched him bury the body, retrieved it after he had departed and hid it somewhere else. Determined to find it, he dug through the entire mountain of garbage, he scoured the ravine floor, he inched up and down the walls. Nothing. Nothing.

It was dark when he returned to the long house. Aunt said sternly: "I don't want you out after dark alone."

Isaac declared dully: "He is gone."

Aunt said nothing, but Isaac felt she knew what had happened. He asked around. A woman said she heard the heavy rain had made the creek swift and it had carried the body away. Another woman said she was told that an evil spirit had stolen the body. Some boys said that braves had taken the body and eaten it. Isaac fell asleep weeping, weeping because the human remains of his friend, made venerable by martyrdom, were evidently lost forever and would be denied a proper respect.

In the morning, Aunt announced: "The hunting is soon to begin. I have arranged that you should accompany the party of my cousin."

"Whatever you wish," Isaac submitted indifferently.

The hunting party was ready in two days and Jogues left the village with it. He felt safe because he was with Aunt's cousin, but he soon perceived that others in the group were not happy to have him along. He was given the heaviest bundles to carry, and when the party ascended high into the mountains to the south, where the snow was deep, he was not provided with snowshoes and had to struggle through the hip-deep drifts. He lagged behind. They warned him that unless he kept the pace they would leave him to die.

One morning they reached a river across which lay a tree trunk, as a bridge. In the party were several women, whose job it would be to skin the animals the men caught and smoke the meat for use later in the winter, and one woman carried a papoose on her back. As she crossed on the log, she lost her balance and fell into the river. Isaac threw his bundles aside and plunged in after the woman, rescuing her and the baby. With that, the attitude of the hunting party measurably changed. Aunt's cousin halted the march while a fire was built for the woman and child to dry themselves. Some food was prepared and Aunt's cousin invited Jogues to sit next to him during the meal. For this, Isaac was grateful, but he was even more grateful for an opportunity which arose in a few hours. The shock of the freezing water was too much for the baby; clearly the infant was dying. Isaac squeezed some water from his clothes, and, pretending to pat the baby affectionately, baptized it a few moments before its death. He began to feel like a missionary again.

They reached the camp site. After helping to erect the tents and fetching firewood, there was not much for Isaac to do. Hunting was considered the duty and honor of men, and the Mohawks did not look upon the Blackrobe as a man. Even the women didn't want him around. During the days that followed, therefore, Isaac had only to collect the firewood twice a day and melt snow to water for cooking and drinking, and then he had his free time for prayers. In the woods, about a mile from the camp, he cleared the snow from a small place, and, using evergreen boughs, built an oratory where he could conduct his spiritual exercises. By going there each day, he was able to make his annual retreat, an experience he thought he would never have again.

The hunting was good at first. There was plenty of meat to eat, plenty more to take back to Ossernenon. To protect their luck, the braves began to gather in a circle each morning and chant implorations to the spirits, asking for continued good fortune. Because of this, Isaac decided that he would eat no more of the meat which, in all likelihood, was being provided by Satan. Aunt's cousin noticed that Isaac had stopped eating the meat and asked him what was wrong. "Nothing," Isaac answered evasively, "I have just lost my taste for it. I am content with the mush." Aunt's cousin shrugged. These Frenchmen were crazy.

Then the luck changed. All the animals seemed to leave the mountains. Day after day, the hunters returned with nothing, unable to understand what had gone wrong. Had they angered the spirits? They chanted more than they had before; they offered sacrifices. Still no animals. What was responsible? Who?

Father Jogues was in his oratory one afternoon when the Mohawks stalked in on him. Infuriated to find him at prayer, they went back to their old ways with him. He was watched constantly to keep him from praying, he was forced to sleep outside tents in the freezing mountain cold, he was permitted only one handful of corn mush at each meal, he could expect to be kicked or struck by anybody who passed near him. All this would be bad enough in the village, but here in the mountains it was an icy agony.

He was therefore almost as relieved as he was stunned when one day an Ossernenon brave arrived at the camp and disclosed that Couture was dying and that he was asking for Isaac. That this concern for a dying Frenchman was extremely unusual for a Mohawk did not occur to Isaac.

Aunt's cousin said: "Good, take this one back to the village. He has been nothing but trouble." He said to Isaac: "You might as well serve some purpose on your trip. Carry these four quarters of deer." It was a load big enough for two men. Aunt's cousin paused, thinking, then he pointed to three women. "You can go back, too. Take some of the bundles. The rest of us can manage what is left."

On the trip, Jogues noticed that the Mohawk who had summoned him seemed annoyed to have the women along. Perhaps they were slowing him down, Isaac figured. Whatever the cause, the man scarcely spoke during the entire journey back, which, because of fresh snowstorms, took over a week. The last day, the brave did not even wait for Isaac and the women, but hurried ahead alone.

[143]

When Jogues reached the village, he put the deer meat in Aunt's cousin's cabin, then went to look for one of the Christian Huron prisoners. "I am going to Tionontoguen," he said. "My brother there is dying."

The Huron looked surprised. "What is wrong with him?"

"I don't know, but he is asking for me. Say some prayers, please."

"He must have been struck very suddenly," the Huron said. "He seemed all right when he was here two days ago."

"Two days ago?"

"Yes. He passed through with a hunting party, going back to Tionontoguen."

"Was he all right then?"

"He had a frozen foot, but that is nothing."

Puzzled, Isaac asked himself aloud: "How can this be? The brave who brought the news must have been at least four or five days on the path when he reached our camp more than a week ago. And you say that two days ago——"

"Which brave?" the Huron asked. Jogues saw the man entering a cabin and pointed him out. The Huron said: "That one? Oh. I heard him in the long house some nights ago, holding a powwow with his friends. They were talking against you. That one said if he ever found you alone anywhere he would know how to take care of you. But I thought it was just talk."

Evidently it was more than talk. The whole thing had been a trap. If Father Jogues had left the camp alone with the brave, he would be dead now. Unwittingly, Aunt's cousin had saved Isaac's life by pausing for a second thought and deciding to send the three women home. The brave could not kill Isaac in front of witnesses; they would tell Aunt, and the brave would be killed for what he had done to Aunt's property. No wonder the brave had been so silent, so angry.

The Huron asked: "Are you going to Tionontoguen?"
"No," Jogues said.
"Do you still want me to pray for your brother?"
"Yes, by all means. And pray for *me*."

CHAPTER NINE

1

AUNT HAD gone to the western mountains with her own hunting party, and because she was away she was made part of another plot against the priest. Isaac's difficult days with Aunt's cousin and then the strain of the quick trip back to Ossernenon had left him exhausted. The second morning while Jogues was resting in Aunt's cabin, an Andagaron brave arrived with a message from her.

"Her party has run out of corn," the brave told Isaac. "She wants you to bring her a fresh supply to her camping place in the mountains."

As weary as he was, Isaac packed a quantity of corn into a heavy bundle, strapped it to his back and slowly trudged out of the village. For no one else but Aunt would he undertake such an ordeal; Aunt he could not refuse. Each step he took sent pains through his aching body as he crossed the plateau and went down to the path which paralleled the river. The morning was very cold. He had gone perhaps half a mile when suddenly a question struck him: "How did Aunt know I was home?" The news could not have traveled that fast to her; her orders could not have reached him so quickly. So it was another trick, another effort to get him away from the village, away from witnesses. He stopped. He was alone on the path. The wind was high and brisk in the trees. He turned and retraced his steps as quickly as he could. He was crossing the plateau to the village when he saw several braves leave the gate. Surprised by the sight of him, they approached him angrily.

The Andagaron brave asked: "Why are you coming back? Did you forget something?"

"No," Isaac said. "I cannot make the trip. I am too tired. I am sick."

The brave who had come to the mountains said: "You must go. The woman has ordered it. She owns you and you must do what she says."

How cleverly they had planned it. "I am sick," Isaac said. "Aunt loves me and will understand why I cannot travel."

A third brave said: "They have no food. They will all be angry with you for leaving them out there without anything to eat."

"They probably have some meat they can eat," Isaac said. "I am not going." Children came out of the village and began to play in the snow, thus providing witnesses. Jogues walked away from the braves, his muscles tense, ready for the tomahawk, but the braves merely muttered curses at him. He went back to Aunt's house and made a fire, stretched out near it and fell asleep. He was safe here. They would not dare touch him inside the house. For the next two weeks he left the cabin only when he could hear the nearby voices of others in the village streets.

It was not necessary for Isaac to tell Aunt what had happened. The Ossernenon women, who loved gossip, told her everything in the short distance from the village gate to her cabin. "I will fix them," Aunt assured Isaac. "I will go to the great-chief and tell him all this and he will punish these men."

Jogues suggested: "If you tell the chief and the men are punished they will be all the more determined to get rid of me. It is better that we forget it. You are home now; they will not try again."

Aunt considered the suggestion, then: "As you wish it,

Nephew. But from now on neither of us should leave the village without the other."

Spring came, and with it came important councils of the leaders of the five nations that comprised the Iroquois federation. The previous summer on the warpath had been a good one; they voted to send out war parties another year. They were afraid of nothing now. Last year they had captured Frenchmen, they had eaten famous Huron warriors, they seized valuable booty, and this inspired them to greater audacity. They planned to attack Sainte Marie and Montreal: they would also attack the fort that now stood at the place where their river entered the St. Lawrence. In this way, they confidently believed, they could conquer both their Indian and French enemies at the same time—once and for all.

During a council, couriers ran in with news: approaching was a band of Sokokis, a small but fierce tribe in the north who were engaged in a long feud with their Algonquin cousins. The feud made the Sokokis and the Iroquois tacit allies. A proper welcome was prepared, and after the formal greetings, the exchange of gifts and the smoking of the pipes, a Mohawk chief asked the Sokoki leader why he had come.

"We are here," the Sokoki said, "because of the Frenchman, the Blackrobe called Ondessonk."

"What about him?"

"Last winter, in a battle with the Algonquins, our best warrior was captured," related the Sokoki. "He was taken to the village near Three Rivers and Quebec, where he was shown off and paraded about and beaten. The time came for him to be killed and to be made a feast for the Algonquins, but the Blackrobes went to them and said they should not do this thing. The Blackrobes saved our warrior's life; they saved him, too, from slavery, for they convinced the Algonquins to release him to us. And we made an agreement."

"And what was that?" the Mohawk asked.

The Sokoki said: "They gave us much wampum and many gifts to bring here to you." On his signal, the wampum and gifts were brought forward. "We are to give you these things in exchange for the man and we are to escort him back to his brothers."

Next morning, after holding a secret powwow, the Mohawks were required to give their response, and the chief said: "The Frenchmen are very generous. We accept their gifts. But is is not necessary for you to escort Ondessonk back to his brothers. We will do that. We already discussed returning him before you arrived. Tell the Frenchmen that we will take Ondessonk back to them in a short time, after our crops have been planted and we are free to travel."

"But it was agreed that we should bring him back," the Sokoki pointed out.

"We captured him; we will free him," the Mohawk said.

The Sokoki was displeased. "If we return without him, we break the agreement."

"We will keep the agreement for you," said the Mohawk, and he stood up, indicating that the discussion was over. The Sokoki knew there was nothing more he could do and he led his men out of Ossernenon.

To Isaac Jogues, this was familiar deception. A similar promise had been made to the Dutch, months before, but nothing was done about it. Nothing would be done about it this time either, he was sure. He would die in this place.

2

The snow melted and filled the rivers; spring rains softened the ground; the sun stayed long in the sky and warmed the fields. Every morning the women left the village to go out and plant their crops, and every morning Isaac followed Aunt to her acres and he worked at her side. One day a boy who was playing nearby looked up at Jogues appraisingly and said: "I know where your friend is."

"My friend?" Isaac asked. "Which friend?"

"The one who died. The one you sought in the ravine."

"You know where he is?"

"What will you give me if I tell you?"

"I have nothing. I am a slave."

This was a fact and it dampened the boy. "You must have something."

Isaac's only possessions were his reading matter, the *Epistle of St. Paul to the Hebrews* and the *Imitation of Christ*. He took them from his shirt. "I have these."

They were not much use. "What would I do with them?" the boy asked.

"You could read them, as I do."

"I don't know how to do that."

"You could come to Aunt's house in the evening and I will show you how."

The boy accepted the offer with a dissatisfied shrug, then said: "Your friend is in the ravine."

"But I searched the ravine. Where?"

"On the far side of the creek. Part-way up the wall are some bushes. They hide a small cave. He is in there."

"Are you certain?"

"I saw him."

Aunt had heard. Isaac gave her a look which asked permission for him to go and see for himself. She turned her back, her way of showing he could go if he wished but she would rather he didn't; he ought not go about alone. Isaac watched the old woman's back for a few moments, then hurried softly away.

The ravine was quiet and deserted. Although it was a garbage dump, there was something cathedral about it, with tall pine and spruce springing from its slanting walls and along its lips, thereby seeming taller and more commanding. Here a man's own breath was too much sound. A footfall among last autumn's leaves was like the rustle of a cassock in a midnight church. Isaac entered the ravine by the slow, curving decline that wound gently away from the plateau like a private road to a hidden monastery. Indeed this was a place for prayers: René Goupil was here. Father Jogues went to the creek and studied the wall that rose sharply from its far bank. The soil was black and wet, the watermark high from the spring flood. Isaac could not determine which cluster of bushes hid the cave that was Goupil's grave: it was necessary for him to wade across the waist-deep creek to examine closer. Then he found it. It was more of a socket left behind by a fallen rock. In it, Jogues discovered a few large bones and several small ones. And there was a skull. He examined the skull carefully. In its crown were two gashes clearly made by a sharp instrument—a tomahawk. Yes, this was René. Isaac kissed the skull tenderly and said some prayers to the dear man whose remains it was. On the bones Jogues recognized the teeth marks of dogs, and he could identify other places where sharp knives had scraped the flesh away. Apparently the Mohawks had eaten him and thrown leftovers to the dogs. Why they had bothered to hide his few remains in this inaccessible place Isaac could not imagine, but he was grateful they did. He had them now and would bury them in a safer place only he would know. He glanced around the ravine and chose a site. Half an hour later he was back on the pathway, striding away from the ravine, confident that he had hidden the bones well, that no one would ever find them. And no one ever did.

Aunt was waiting for him on the plateau, actually guarding him so that no one would go into the ravine after him; she walked back to the village with him. From the attitude he bore, she knew that he had done whatever it was he wanted to do, but she did not want to discuss it with him. Instead, she said: "It will soon be time for us to take our furs to the Dutchmen to trade. I want you to come with me."

He said: "Yes, Aunt."

"Will you like that—being among the Dutchmen for a few days?"

"Yes, Aunt."

"It is not a bad trip," she said. "A man could walk it in two days."

He glanced at her, wondering why she had said that. "Are we going to walk it?"

"No. We will go by canoe. But it is not a bad walk for anyone who would care to make it. There are no villages along the way, nothing, nobody."

Was she hinting that he might try to escape? Not once in almost a year of slavery had the possibility occurred to him. He had so adjusted himself to death at the hands of the Mohawks that the expectation of anything else had vanished completely from his mind. The thought of freedom weakened him briefly, but then he dismissed the idea. Escape was impossible; he could not achieve it alone and anybody who helped him would be in serious trouble. Furthermore, with Couture still a slave and the Christian Hurons still slaves, escape was unthinkable. These people needed him.

Aunt's group left a week later. Compared to the annual Huron trek, this was no journey at all, just forty miles, and even at a casual pace the trip could be made in two days. There was a small flotilla, four or five canoes. Because of the proximity of Rensselaerswyck, the Mohawks did not make a big project out of the trading. The various Mohawk hunting teams would take their furs to the Dutch whenever they felt like it over the next few weeks, until it was time for the annual fishing trips.

News of Isaac's arrival had rushed through the settlement. Arendt Van Corlaer hurried to the riverside to meet him: so had the town officials; so had the Dominie Johannes Megapolensis, the Dutch Reformed minister, who invited him to dinner. When Aunt had announced that she was taking him to Rensselaerswyck, the Ossernenon chiefs insisted that extra braves go along as guards to keep an eye on him, and even now, in the Dominie's dining room, three braves stood along the wall watching him put into his mouth the bread and mashed potatoes and roast and gravy—things he thought he would never taste again.

Isaac found it strange to be speaking French again, strange to sit in a chair, strange to take a European meal at a table that was covered with linen and lined with silverware. Because of his mangled hands he manipulated his knife and fork awkwardly, but the loss of the habit made him even clumsier. "I am afraid I am out of practice," he apologized when his fork again slipped from his fingers.

The Dutchmen at the table smiled with patient understanding. The Dominie said: "After dinner, I have something else for you that I suspect you have lost the practice of."

The Dutchmen questioned him about his year of slavery, shaking their heads when he told them of what had happened to him, what he had seen happen to others. Van Corlaer said: "I tried every way I knew to buy your freedom, but the chiefs wouldn't hear of it."

"I know," Isaac said. "I am grateful."

"And I was a fool," Van Corlaer went on, "to believe for a minute that they would actually take you back to Three Rivers as a peace offering."

"I knew they wouldn't," said Isaac. "Sometimes I wonder what on earth they are saving me for." He told them about the Sokokis. "I am sure that if ever I see Three Rivers again it will not be because the Mohawks arranged it."

They finished their dinner and went into the sitting room, the Mohawk braves following. Dominie Megapolensis disappeared for a moment, then returned carrying a book. Isaac recognized it from across the room. "My breviary! I have missed it more than I miss my fingers."

Megapolensis gave it to Jogues. "I've had it only a few weeks. Some traders brought it from Ossernenon. I guess it has been there all the time."

The Jesuit flipped through its pages lovingly. "If I had had it I would not have been so lonely. Now I can pray again. I can never thank you enough, Dominie."

"Yes, you can," the minister said. "Say my name once in a while when you are reading it." He sat down. "Now, let's talk about your escape."

"Escape?" Isaac said the word almost sadly. "Impossible!"

"Of course it is possible," assured Van Corlaer. "We will hide you."

With a movement of his head, Isaac indicated the three braves along the wall. "Do you think these men will let me out of their sight for a moment? One wrong move and they will be on my neck."

"We can do something," the Dominie insisted. "You should be here another day or two. We will discuss it among ourselves and let you know what we decide. Meanwhile, is there anything else we can do for you?"

"I would like to write a report to my Superiors in France," Isaac said. "Can you arrange to have it delivered?"

"Yes."

"And I would like to write a letter to my mother."

"Yes, of course. A ship will be here in a few weeks. We can arrange everything."

"You can have anything you want," said Van Corlaer,

"but just remember that you may not be going back to Ossernenon, and if we can't prevent that on this trip we will arrange to get you out of there at the first opportunity."

Isaac gave them a sad and knowing smile. It would never happen.

3

He was back at Ossernenon in four days, not particularly disappointed that he had not escaped, because he never seriously thought he would. Couture came to see him, and Isaac related his experiences at Rensselaerswyck.

"You will escape, Father," Couture said. "I'm sure of it."

"It's not that important," said Jogues. "Yes, I would like to get away, if only to go somewhere I would be permitted to live and work like a missionary again. But I don't want to involve the Dutch. If they helped me escape the Mohawks would surely attack them. And if I escaped on my own, there would be you Guillaume. They would kill you in reprisal."

"Don't worry about me, Father. I have had many chances to escape this past year, but I didn't take them because of you. Think about yourself. The instant I learn you are gone I will be on my way."

Jogues shrugged. "There are the others. Theresa."

"Theresa is all right. She is not even treated like a slave any more. You know how it is, Father. These people absorb each other after a while. Theresa is behaving as beautifully as she always did, but I would not be surprised if she took a Mohawk as a husband one of these days."

The priest scoffed. "How could she do that? She is a Christian. She could not marry without a priest, without me there. No, Guillaume, I cannot think of escaping. I am needed here."

Couture turned impatient. "Father, supposing it had been you who was killed instead of René? The rest of us would have managed somehow to remain good Christians, until we either died or found another priest. And we will manage, too, if you are able to escape. You must think of yourself, Father. You have gone through enough for us. How you must yearn to be able to say Mass again!"

"With these?" He held up his hands. "I doubt that it would be permitted." But he was touched by Couture's concern. "I will decide what to do when the time comes, if it ever does."

Two circumstances kept Ossernenon busy, the forthcoming fishing season and the resumption of the war. By early summer, Mohawk bands were already roaming through the Huron country, burning villages, killing, taking prisoners and bringing them back for torture and for the flames. Occasionally Jogues was able to get to the Christian Hurons, hear their confessions and prepare them for death; occasionally he was able to baptize some of the pagans. Then he was forced to witness the torture, the killing, the fires, and he wept because there was nothing he could do to prevent all this or to hasten its cruel end.

The Mohawks were extravagantly brazen. They attacked Montreal and brought back eleven prisoners. They attacked the 1644 Huron flotilla, en route to Three Rivers, killing most of the travelers, bringing back fifteen prisoners and the valuable booty of the winter's furs. They also brought back the Jesuit documents that were to be sent to France, and because these things were useless to them, they gave the papers to Isaac. He read a report about his capture and discovered that the Jesuits at Sainte Marie thought he was dead.

The important Mohawk war plan for the summer was to be an attack on the fort at the junction of the Richelieu and the St. Lawrence rivers. The fort posed crippling obstacles to the Mohawks. To avoid it, they had either to go the last miles to the St. Lawrence overland, which was difficult, or try to sneak past the fort at night, which was dangerous. The fort would have to be destroyed. The trouble was that the Mohawks could not determine the size of the attack force they would need. The fort was well constructed; cannons peered over the palisade, but the decisive factor would be the number of French soldiers in the fort, and the Mohawks did not know. Somehow they must find out. The war chiefs summoned Father Jogues.

"We have decided," their spokesman said, "that it is time for you to return to your brothers."

Jogues said: "That is very good of you."

"But we want to be sure," the man said, "that the French are ready to talk peace with us."

"I can understand that," said Isaac, but not believing it.

"We want you to take the paper and the quill the Dutch gave you and write a message to the commander of the fort on the big river and tell him that he is to hold council with us to decide on the terms of the peace. You are to say that the council is to be held inside the fort."

Isaac said: "I shall do it. When do you want the message?"

"In the morning."

That night, Isaac sat near the fire in Aunt's house and wrote the message. Aware that the Mohawks probably distrusted him and might give the message to someone to be read back to them—a cunning trader or some renegade Huron prisoner who, taught to read at a mission, might bargain to read the letter in exchange for his freedom—Isaac wrote it in a blend of French, Latin, Greek and Huron, beginning a sentence with one language and ending it in another. Thus he felt no Indian would be able to read enough of it, no poorly schooled trader would be able to read much of it, but an educated man, an army officer

[157]

or another priest, would be able to read it all, and Isaac presumed that with the priest or the officer the news would be safe. He wrote what he suspected was the Mohawk plan, suggesting:

"Those who present this message to you will be spies, sent to count you and your weapons, and if their leaders are dissatisfied with the estimate they will agree to a council in order to get inside the fort to count for themselves. When they know your strength, they will know the size of the force they need to conquer you. Only by quelling the planned attack early will you possibly assure your defense and perhaps even put an end to the Mohawk warpath. Pay no attention to any proposals to make peace on an offer of my freedom. It will never be given to me and you will only endanger yourselves further."

Next morning he gave the message to the war chiefs. A while later, he saw the bands of Mohawk braves in full war regalia leave the village, and during the rest of the day he watched similar bands from other villages pass below on the river path. He was certain that warriors from the villages of other Iroquois tribes were also making their way to the fort, perhaps for an immediate attack if the fort was under strength.

Meanwhile, the fishing season arrived. Just as there had been winter hunting parties, now there would be summer fishing parties. Aunt told Isaac Jogues she would take him with her group. Her favorite fishing spot was in the Hudson River, some twenty miles below Rensselaerswyck, where the river widened into shallows thick with reeds.

They left a week after the warriors had departed from the village, and the next evening they were at Rensselaerswyck, where they decided to spend the night. Two braves accompanied Jogues on a visit to the Dominie.

The Dominie asked: "Did you see the big ship anchored in the river?"

"Yes, I did," said Isaac.

"It leaves in a few days for New Amsterdam, then on to Europe. You can be on it," offered the Dominie. "I have already spoken to the captain."

"Within one hour after the ship left, the Mohawks would set fire to your town," Isaac predicted.

"The ship brought us fresh troops. We are well fortified. The Mohawks don't attack when they think they might lose."

"I am not worth a war," Jogues said, "even the risk of one."

The Dominie assured him. "The captain is determined to take you. He was appalled when I told him what you had been through."

"Those days are past," Isaac said hopefully.

At the edge of the town was the small farm of a Dutchman who had married a Mohawk squaw, and it was here, in the barn, that visiting Mohawks usually slept. The Mohawks had also seen the big ship in the river; when it was time to sleep they took Isaac to the barn and saw to it that he slept far back from the door.

Impatient to get on with the fishing, Aunt led her group to the spot she had chosen, a day's trip south of the Dutch settlement. A few tents were erected and a small cabin was built, then the group was ready for the fishing. The nets were put out at intervals; the Mohawk method was to drag the nets to shore at specified times, thus hauling in the catch. The fishing was good; the Mohawks smoked great quantities for use in the winter. Occasionally news came down the river, and the news from Ossernenon was bleak. War parties were bringing in Huron and Algonquin prisoners every day, torturing them, killing them, eating them.

The news sickened Isaac. He said: "Aunt, permit me to go back to the village. You do not need me here."

She was not deluded; he wanted to go back to his Christians. "All right," she said. "Go. Be careful. Good-by." She had never said good-by to him before.

4

She appointed two braves to paddle the canoe for him and they were at Rensselaerswyck the next afternoon. Their approach attracted attention on the shore, and as they neared the bank Isaac Jogues observed an unusual number of Mohawks, waiting. He stepped ashore. Immediately the crowd jumped on him, beating him, kicking him, whipping him. It was worse than a gauntlet because there was no end of the line. Moreover, Isaac had no idea why he was being punished. Finally the Dutch were able to struggle their way through the mob to Isaac and isolate him for a little while.

The Dominie said: "There was a big attack on a French fort on the St. Lawrence, but it failed. Apparently the French started to fight before the Indians were ready. Scores of Iroquois have been killed. They blame you for it."

"They are right," Isaac admitted.

The Mohawks reclaimed Isaac and took him to the barn where they held him prisoner while word was sent to Ossernenon. Meanwhile, the Mohawks kept the Dutch away from Isaac. The Dominie could speak to him only by shouting into the barn in French.

"You know you are doomed," he called to Isaac. "They will kill you now, for sure."

"I know it," Isaac replied.

"We can still save you."

"It is too late."

"The ship is still here; the captain is still willing to take you aboard."

"It is too dangerous for you."

"Let us decide that."

Isaac had so adjusted himself to death that he considered no alternative. "I must do God's Will."

"Of course you must, but His Will may be that should escape. You won't know unless you try."

This was true. "What shall I do?"

Carefully, the Dominie said: "During the night, you must make your way out of this barn. About a half-mile up the road, there is a big elm. A boat has been put there for you. Row out to the ship. They will be expecting you."

"I will try."

Night came and the Mohawks gathered in the barn for sleep. They bolted the door to prevent Jogues from attempting an escape, but they did not think of setting up a guard.

Isaac waited until he heard the Indians snoring. He got up carefully and cautiously and inched his way to the door where, with excruciating patience, he slid back the bolt and lifted the crosspiece. He opened the door a crack at a time, slipped through the narrow opening he made for himself, then slowly closed the door behind him. He moved away, as lightly as the Indians walked, away from the barn toward the road.

He heard the nearby growl of a farm dog. He took a few steps. Another growl came on the other side, closer. Now he heard more dogs running up, stopping suddenly to sniff him from a distance. The dogs did not know him and they grew nervous, whimpering, uttering soft threatening barks. Isaac had no choice: he would have to make a run for it.

The dogs were on him, snarling, barking, biting, as Jogues struggled to escape them. The Dutch farmer ran from the house with his musket. The barn door burst open and the Mohawks tore out. It was all over in a few moments.

Isaac had been bitten twice on the legs, bad bites. He had not experienced such pain since his thumb was cut off. The only treatment available was to wash the wounds and bandage them. Angry Mohawks stood by while this was done by the farmer, then they took Isaac back to the barn. This time they secured the door not only with the bolt but with their bodies, several of them sleeping against the door so that it could not be opened without arousing them. Other Mohawks slept in a circle around Jogues; he would have to step over them to get away, and they slept lightly enough to be awakened by this.

The night moved on. Isaac's pain was too great for him to sleep, but greater was the pain of knowing that his attempt to escape had failed. Why hadn't he stopped to think about the dogs? They had not bothered him during the day. If he had talked to them softly, tried to pet them, they might have lost their night fears and let him pass. It was too late now. He would soon be dead.

Hours later, he became aware of a strange sound, and he thought it was rats. Then he recognized the sound: a door was being opened. He looked around. At the back of the barn, hidden by stalls, was a small door, and someone was opening it. Movement was difficult for Jogues, with the sleeping Mohawks pressed against him, but slowly he made his way free, arose, stepped carefully over the braves, and crept to the hidden door.

The black night was fading to predawn purple as Father Jogues stepped outside. He recognized the face of a farm-hand. The man beckoned. Isaac put his mouth to the man's ear and whispered: "The dogs?" The man shook his head. No dogs. Then the farmhand gestured to indicate that the way was clear, that Isaac should go quickly.

Fifteen minutes later, Isaac Jogues came upon the rowboat under the elm. He gave it a push to set it afloat, but it was caught in the mud. Anguish filled him as he shoved and pulled and dug into the mud, but still the boat would not budge. He wondered if all these obstacles could be God's way of showing that he was not to escape. He tried the boat again. This time it gave an inch, then another, another. And finally it was free. Quickly, Isaac climbed aboard and rowed out to the ship. The men on watch had been alerted for him and when they saw him coming they lowered a rope ladder over the side and he climbed it.

When Jogues stepped on deck, no one dared speak, for fear that the clear morning air might carry the sounds to shore. The crewmen signaled Isaac to follow them. They led him below-deck, deeper and deeper into the ship, to a trap door that opened to the bilge, and they indicated that he should descend into the dark, wet, stinking pit. One said: "I'll get the captain." And they closed the door over him.

There was no room for him to stand; he rested by leaning against the few steps that came from the trap door. In a few minutes the door was pulled open, then:

"This is the captain. Are you all right?"

"Yes, Captain. I'm all right."

"I'm sorry to have to put you down there, but it's the only safe place we have."

"I don't mind, Captain." The stench of the scummy bilge water sickened him.

"As soon as I get clearance from the commandant of the fort, we'll shove off."

"Very good."

"We'll have you out of there in a few hours."

"Very good."

He was in the bilge fifty hours, unable to stand or sit, unable to eat or sleep. At last, he was brought on deck. The Dominie was there, Van Corlaer, the commandant, and the

[163]

captain, and the news was bad. The Mohawks had scoured the town, the woods, the river for Isaac, and they were now convinced he was on the ship. The captain refused to let them make a search, which convinced them even further, and they had threatened that unless the Blackrobe was turned over to them they would burn the town, kill everyone in it, and they would somehow board the ship and hunt out Isaac even if a fight cost them every Mohawk in the tribe.

"There is no question, then," said Jogues. "I must give myself up."

"No, you don't," said the captain. "We can be under sail in a half-hour, and we're going to do it."

"At the risk of others' lives? No. Take me ashore. I will give myself up."

"You don't have to do that," said Van Corlaer, "but we must get you off this ship so that Mohawks can search it. You can come back later."

Isaac shook his head; he had had enough.

The commandant said: "I have already let them search my quarters and they know you are not there. I have an attic. You can hide out there for a while."

Submissively, hopelessly, Father Jogues allowed himself to be taken off the ship to the attic of the commandant's house at the fort. He was there twelve days, and in a way it was a worse prison cell than the bilge. Again there was no room for him to stand, little room for him to move; and because the Mohawks walked in and out of the Dutch homes as casually as though they were village long houses, Isaac dared not move at all for fear he might be heard below by an uninvited Mohawk visitor. The thatched roof caught all the sun's full heat, baking Isaac by day and night, and when it rained Isaac might just as well have been standing in an open field.

The big ship was searched, then ordered to sail immediately. Reaching New Amsterdam, the captain reported the events at Rensselaerswyck. Director-General Willem Kieft, in charge of the entire Dutch colony, would tolerate no more indecision or delay. "Frenchman or not, we've got to get the man out of there," he declared. He ordered a shallop to Rensselaerswyck, with instructions that if it did not bring back the priest in a week he would go north himself after Isaac and see to it at the same time that there was a change in authority there.

When the small sailing vessel arrived, the Dominie, Van Corlaer and the commandant held a conference to determine how they could obey Kieft's orders. Deciding they would have to resort to duplicity, they circulated through the town the rumor that Kieft had sent for them to discuss a way in which the Dutch could help the Mohawks locate Isaac, thus putting an end to the estrangement which had evolved between the Iroquois and the settlers because of him. They would leave the next morning. Van Corlaer asked the Mohawk leaders in town to meet at his house to make their own suggestions for a search for Isaac; most other Mohawks waited outside for the plans. The Mohawks thus occupied at one end of town, the Dutch were able to transfer the priest secretly from the commandant's attic to the shallop and hide him in its shallow hold.

In the morning, the three Dutchmen came to the ship with other town officials, who thought that Kieft had actually sent for them. The leading Mohawks came to the dock for farewells of guarded amiability. The sails were run up, the ship moved out from the dock and nosed slowly southward.

When they were midstream and down-river a few miles, the commandant stepped to the hold and said: "Father?"

Isaac said: "Yes?"

The Dutchmen who had not been part of the scheme were

astounded to find the missing priest aboard the shallop with them.

Van Corlaer said: "You will have to stay down there all day, Father, until we are beyond the Mohawk fishing camps."

"All right."

For safety's sake, he remained in the hold all day. He knew that at some point they would be passing Aunt's camp, and he prayed a good-by to her, grateful for the protection she had given him. He prayed, too, for Couture, for the Christian prisoners of the Mohawks, for the priests at Sainte Marie, for the Dutch who had saved him, for everyone in this great, mysterious land he had come to love so much and now believed he would never see again.

CHAPTER TEN

1

SEVERE STORMS settled over the North Atlantic, that winter of 1643. Captains of ships, expecting trouble, had left their New World ports early. The harbor at New Amsterdam was empty. It looked as though Isaac would have to remain in the Dutch town almost a year, until the big ships arrived from Holland on their annual round trips. Then, in October, a stray Dutch vessel wandered into port, searching for cargo. It was a small craft, scarcely worthy of coastal service, but its hardy crew made a living from gathering up the cargo scraps which had arrived from the inland too late for the bigger ships or were left behind because there was no room. The crew had had some luck in Virginia and were now testing New Amsterdam before attempting the dash across to Holland. The ship had no accommodations for passengers, but the skipper was willing to take Isaac Jogues along if he did not mind living with the crew and giving a hand at the various chores required to keep the vessel afloat. Jogues was ready to do anything in order to be on the move again.

As it turned out, there was enough cargo at New Amsterdam to fill the small ship, even part of the crew's quarters, which meant that Isaac would have to bunk on the open deck. He did not care. On the morning of November 5, the crew hoisted sail and the ship bobbed across the broad harbor, out to the sea, to the waiting storms. With the wind at its stern, the ship made relatively good time, but the sea was high and cruel the whole way. Towering waves swept across the deck. It was impossible for Isaac to get dry. The Dutch clothes which had been given him at New Amsterdam were drenched within an hour after leaving the port, and he remained soaked to the skin for almost eight weeks. Deck cargo, its ropes broken by the pounding seas, slid down at him. He did not dare to sleep, for fear he would be crushed to death before he had time to say a prayer. And he did not get much chance for sleep. Each time the angry, cursing, disgruntled crew was sent to repair the damage, Isaac had to take his place in line, lifting, shoving, roping.

At the end of December's third week, the weary vessel nosed into the English Channel. The worst was over. Then the cry went up: *Pirates!* Two buccaneer ships were coming up fast from the south, their cannons already blazing. The skipper of the tiny Dutch vessel had only the defense of flight. He veered his ship to port and made for the Bay of Falmouth. Once there, the crew made a decision: rather than risk again the storm and the pirates, they would remain in England until a safer day, regardless of when that might be. But what about the priest? The English anti-Catholics were in power again, and if the authorities discovered a priest on the ship they would confiscate the cargo as a punishment for bringing a papal enemy into the country. How to get rid of him? A Dutch collier was anchored in the bay, scheduled to sail for Bordeaux when circumstances allowed; its captain was willing to take Isaac along, but for safety's sake he insisted that the priest come aboard only at the last minute. Isaac remained on the small ship on which he had crossed the Atlantic. Late one night, when most of the crew was ashore, English wharf-bandits came aboard. Aware that one word from him would reveal his nationality, thus his religion, Isaac stood by helplessly as the bandits ransacked the crew's quarters and then, for good measure, relieved him of his hat and overcoat. He was freezing when, hours later, the skipper returned and, learning what happened, denounced Isaac as the bearer of bad luck, blaming him for the storm, the pirates, the robbery, and ordering him off the ship.

Fortunately, word arrived that the collier would sail at dawn; Isaac went aboard, where he was hidden in the coal-filled hold. He was there, at his prayers, when he realized the date: it was December 24, the vigil of Christmas, the eve of the birth of the Saviour, the eve of Isaac's own re-birth.

Late in the day, the captain sent for him. "We're safe away from England now. You can stay on deck, unless some English Navy ship comes alongside to make an inspection."

Isaac said: "I am grateful to you, Captain. I know what a chance you are taking."

"I have no love for the English," the captain said, dismissing Isaac's gratitude. "Our port is Bordeaux. I imagine you can make your way home from there?"

Remaining aboard until Bordeaux meant missing Christmas ashore. "You won't be touching France sooner?"

"I have no such plans. Why?"

"My home is in the north."

The captain glanced at his charts. "We'll be off the Breton coast in the morning. We can put you ashore there, if you like."

"Thank you, Captain."

Jogues remained awake the whole night, enraptured by the confidence that when morning came he would go ashore and find a church where he could receive the Sacraments for the first time in seventeen months—on Christmas Day.

The early morning was still dark, the air clear and very cold, when the captain sent for Isaac and told him to get ready. "We're about two miles out," he said. "My men will take you ashore in a rowboat. I believe there is a village at this point."

"Thank you, Captain," Isaac said, "and a merry Christmas."

"And to you. Here, you'll need these." The Captain handed Isaac a heavy coat and a cap, both much too large but both warming.

The fishing village was small, and there were lights in just one or two houses when Jogues stepped from the rowboat to the tiny dock. Standing in a doorway was a man who watched Isaac Jogues land; a moment later, the priest noticed him and went to him.

Isaac asked: "Is there a church nearby that has Mass at this point."

"There's a Recollet monastery on the other side of town," said the man. "They have Masses all morning."

"Thank you. I will go there."

"I saw you land."

"Yes?"

"Where did you come from?"

"From England."

The man grunted his disapproval of the English. "You're lucky to be out of there alive."

Eager to hurry on to the monastery, Father Jogues made no comment.

The man took in Isaac's ill-fitting clothes with a half-smile. "You ought to dress up when you go to Mass on Christmas morning." He slipped off his red scarf and tied it around Jogues's neck. "There, that's better."

The priest was touched by the stranger's kindness, and he smiled. "Thank you very much."

"This is my home," the man said. "Come back after Mass and have breakfast with my family."

"I will."

Only a few villagers were in the church for the dawn

Mass. As he entered, Isaac saw a priest go into a confessional; quickly he was at the man's elbow giving an account of his life since his last confession; it seemed forever ago. Then he took his place in the church and witnessed the beautiful Christmas Mass that commemorated the birth of the Infant for whose sake Isaac had so willingly undergone the torments of the past months. When he received the Host, Jogues felt that he was also receiving his own life again.

A half-hour later, Isaac was again at the home of the man who had given him the scarf. The family was up now, preparing for Mass in the village church, and as the wife took time to prepare a breakfast for the stranger, the children showed him their gifts. Then the man noticed Isaac's hands. "The English did *that* to you?"

"No," Isaac said evasively.

"Who did?"

"Indians."

"The savages in the New World?"

"Yes. Indians."

Astonished, the man asked: "Who are you?" Deep concern. "Who *are* you, sir?"

There was no escape. "I am a Jesuit missionary," Jogues admitted. "I have been in New France seven years. This is my first day home."

The news raced through the village and quickly the house was full of people, full of questions. Jogues found it unpleasant to discuss his experiences in terms of himself, so he related the details of his years in New France in terms of others who had shared his life there with him. His listeners gasped at the atrocities he described, but Isaac assured them firmly that Christian Indians were far different from the pagans and he predicted that one day when all the Indians were Christians, the pagan cruelties would disappear from the country.

A businessman from Rennes, visiting relatives in the village for the holidays, asked: "Where do you go from here, Father?"

"To Paris, to my Superiors. They do not know I'm here."

"When do you go?"

"As soon as I can."

"How do you go?"

"Any way I can. Walk, if I must."

"I shall be returning to Rennes in a few days. I know the Jesuits there. Will you do me the honor of traveling with me?"

"You do me an honor in asking."

They arrived at Rennes very late on January 4, too late for Isaac to go to the Jesuit house; but at five-thirty the next morning, when he knew the priests would be finishing their meditations and preparing for Mass, he was in the quiet street, knocking on the door. A Jesuit lay brother answered it.

"I wish to see the Father Rector," Isaac said.

In his borrowed clothes, Jogues looked like a beggar. "He is vesting for Mass. You will have to come back later."

"Could I see him now?" Isaac pressed. "I have some news for him from New France."

"Come in. I will tell him." He showed Isaac into a small, bare reception room, then went away.

Merely being in a Jesuit establishment again was a great joy. The few chairs, straight and hard, were familiar; the smell of strong soap and wax was wonderfully familiar; the early morning silence, almost a prayerful thing, was gloriously familiar. This was home, for these Jesuits were his brothers. He heard footsteps.

A priest entered. "You want to see me?"

"Father Rector?"

"Yes. You have news from Canada? You know our Fathers there?"

"Yes, I know them."

[172]

"Father Vimont?"

"The Superior—the last to whom I spoke."

"De Brébeuf, Garnier, Lalemant?"

"I know them well."

"Isaac Jogues—did you know him?"

"Oh, yes."

"We have a report that he was captured by the Iroquois and tortured, and that he is dead. Do you know anything about Father Jogues?"

"He is not dead. He stands before you." Isaac held out his hands.

The priest studied the hands and saw upon them the tortures he had read about in Jesuit reports. Dazed, he looked into Isaac's eyes and saw there the plea for recognition and acceptance. "Dear God in Heaven!" He took Isaac into his arms.

2

He was the talk of France. Even before his first letters from Rennes reached his Superiors in Paris and his mother in Orleans, the whole country knew he was alive, that he was free, that he was in comparatively good health, that he was home. He was mobbed when he tried to cross a street, the hierarchy lionized him, journalists begged for a moment of his time, Queen Anne summoned him. He had no peace, no privacy, and he found the ordeal of his popularity more agonizing than running a Mohawk gauntlet. The first time the Queen sent for him, he asked to be excused; her second request was a royal command and he had to go to the Palais Royal to submit himself to her questions and the stares of her court. He was obliged to tell his story so often that it embarrassed him and he frequently left out long portions of it. It pained him to speak about himself so much, and he adopted the habit, even in his official reports, of referring to himself in the third person, so that it was "he" who was beaten, "he" whose fingers were chewed off, "he" who kissed the bones of René Goupil and wept over them.

Isaac hoped he would find solitude in his mother's house, but he did not. All his relatives filed into the house for a look at the family celebrity. Only his brother Samuel, who had become a Capuchin friar, seemed to understand why he had gone through what he had, and when the two priests had their few moments alone together they both experienced an empathy that gave Isaac a bit of comfort, a bit of inner quiet.

Madame Jogues, at the first sight of her favorite child, sobbed over the evidence of his sufferings. But he was home now, and she believed that, in view of all he had suffered, he would be allowed to remain. When, after a few days, she mentioned this to him, he put an arm around her shoulders and the touch of his mutilated hands filled her again with tears. He said: "You gave me to God and the Jesuits, Mother, and you can't take me back." He stepped away and held out his arms, putting himself on display. "Look at me." He was smiling. "Why, I have become a savage myself. These new shoes are killing me and this new soutane makes me feel like something in a shop window. I am as out of place in France as the St. Lawrence River would be. If the Jesuits have any sense at all, they will send me back to the Mohawks where I belong."

"They won't," she said confidently.

"I hope they will. I pray for it," Isaac said, quite serious.

He prayed for something else, too.

The rubrics for Mass clearly described each move, each gesture, each intonation the celebrant was to perform. At one point, he was to hold the Host reverently between his thumbs and forefingers and elevate it. He was also to cup the chalice in his hands in a special way and elevate it.

But Jogues was missing a thumb and his forefingers were stubs. He could not follow the rubrics; he therefore could not say Mass, and one of the great joys of his priesthood was being denied him. This deprivation distressed him more than anything that had happened to him or could happen to him. His Superiors knew how he felt and they took steps to obtain a papal dispensation. To Pope Urban VIII went documents of recommendation signed by the Jesuit Provincial of France, the Father General of the Society in Rome, the French Ambassador to the Vatican, by Queen Anne herself. In March, the Pope responded, saying: "It would be shameful that a martyr of Christ be not allowed to drink the Blood of Christ." The dispensation was granted. Thus, after twenty months of spiritual loneliness, Father Isaac Jogues donned the vestments and approached the altar and was once again a full priest.

The Jesuit Superiors were also aware of Jogues's intense desire to return to the missions, and they were divided in their opinions about it. They agreed that he had suffered enough for one man, for a dozen men, and that it would be inhuman to expose him to the risk of more. Some of the Superiors pointed out that Father Jogues now held a special value to the Society: his knowledge of the languages and mentalities of the Hurons, Algonquins and Mohawks. This knowledge could make him an invaluable teacher in the training of future missionaries, and the men holding this view recommended that Jogues be assigned as a professor in a Jesuit seminary. In the opinion of others, Isaac's wide popularity throughout France had its own value. Through writings and lectures, he could stimulate public interest in the missions, resulting in increased vocations and financial assistance. There was a third view, and it was sympathetically regarded by all the Superiors: Father Jogues wanted to go back to New France and his wish should be granted.

When Isaac Jogues returned to Paris after his brief visit

with his family, he was summoned by Father Jean Filleau, then the French Provincial. Slowly and carefully, Filleau gave Jogues the results of the discussion about his future, first disclosing the recommendations that he teach or write or lecture. As he listened, Isaac's personal hopes painfully withered.

"Lastly," Filleau said, "we considered your wish to go back to New France. We all respect this and admire it, but some of the Fathers felt they could not in conscience accede to this wish because of the certain death that awaits you should you ever again fall into the hands of the Iroquois. In the end, we reached no agreement at all and I have decided to leave the decision to you."

"You know I want to go back, Father Provincial," Jogues said humbly, "but I have a vow of obedience to the Society and so I shall do whatever you say."

Filleau nodded, then picked up a document from his desk and kept his eyes on it as he said: "In the harbor at La Rochelle is a troopship that will be leaving for New France in three weeks. I have received a letter from the captain of the ship, requesting a chaplain." He looked at Jogues. "Would this assignment interest you?"

Isaac was beaming. "Very much."

3

The Jesuits along the St. Lawrence were not certain whether Isaac was dead or alive, or, if alive, where he was. On the basis of rumors that he had escaped from the Mohawks, they assumed that he was with the Dutch at one of the Hudson River settlements, but they were unable to obtain any confirmation of this. During the winter which Jogues had spent in France, his confreres in New France were still praying for his safety. That spring, he was aboard the first ship that came up the river, and the sight of him—alive, in good health, in high spirits—struck Tadoussac, Quebec and then Three Rivers as a miracle.

The three French settlements were in need of a miracle. The five tribes of the Iroquois nation had remained on the warpath for three years, pinning the missionaries down to the villages, preventing travel, preventing trade. The priests at Sainte Marie were completely without supplies; the Hurons dared not wander far from their long houses even to hunt for the meat and fish they desperately needed. In desperation, an attempt had been made to run the Iroquois blockade by sending out a Huron flotilla early in the year, while ice was still on the rivers, but Iroquois war parties were already on the move and the entire flotilla, including Father Francesco Bressani, of the Italian Province, had been captured. There were rumors that the Dutch had ransomed Bressani, but nobody was sure.

As the Iroquois nation had planned while Father Jogues was still a prisoner of the Mohawk tribe, attacks had been made upon Sainte Marie, also Montreal and Three Rivers. The fort which the French had erected at the mouth of the river of the Iroquois, to hold back the war parties, had failed in its purpose and was now abandoned. Every tribe in the area had suffered from the Iroquois fury—the Petuns, the Neutrals, the Algonquins, even the Sokokis who had a peace pact with the Iroquois. But it was the Hurons who suffered worst; slowly but steadily the Iroquois were wiping them out.

The return of Isaac Jogues to New France, the return of the Jesuit who had undergone such torment at the hands of the Iroquois and lived to come back, therefore appeared to symbolize the end of an era, an era of fear, of helplessness, of immobility. His return served as an inspiration to his confreres; his presence revived their zeal; his openly

[177]

announced determination to go back to the Mohawks some day gave them courage and hope.

In the present circumstances, however, Isaac's desire to go back to the Mohawks could be little more than a dream. Because of the dangers in travel, it was impossible for him to go back even to Sainte Marie. Fresh troops from France had secured a measure of safety for the settlers only as far west as Montreal, but beyond Montreal there was no safety at all. Jogues, then, had to content himself with Montreal, where, a few weeks after his return to New France, he settled down as a missionary partner to Father Jacques Buteux, his closest friend during his seminary years.

Isaac Jogues was a happy man again. Although confined to the island of Montreal, his long days were crowded with missionary duties. A score of Christian Algonquins lived at Montreal, and because of them the priests were able to make more effective contacts with the pagans. Father Jogues noticed a change in the pagans since he had last been at Montreal almost two years before. The sullen patience with which they had then listened to him seemed to have mellowed; he had observed a similar mollification among the pagans at Three Rivers and Quebec. True, there had been no unusual acceleration in the number of conversions, but the petulant resistance of the pagans appeared to have given way to an air of guarded interest, as though they were believing what they were told about Christianity while not being sure that they ought to believe. Actually, this subtle change was inevitable; it was a product of the passing years, growing out of the presence and spiritual influence of both the Christian Indians and the priests, and it affected the relationships of pagans among themselves as well as with the Christians and the priests, in that time itself had dissipated the fear of strangers and strange ideas, while, in the same time, bringing about an ineluctable absorption of some of the new ideas. To be sure, in this land where the habits of lust, hate and revenge had deep roots, centuries old, the change after just twenty years of missionary effort could only be a topsoil change, but nevertheless in the change were the seeds of the Christian virtues of mercy, forgiveness and tolerance, from which other virtues could grow. The missionaries knew this, and because of it they were willing to undergo more years of hardship, sacrifice and suffering in their crusade for souls.

Meanwhile the Hurons and the Algonquins, although they were outweighed by the Iroquois in numbers and in weapons, nevertheless did not give up the battle. From time to time, joint bands of them penetrated the forest to search for small groups of Iroquois and attack them. One day in the spring of 1644, such an effort resulted in the capture of three Iroquois. They were taken to Three Rivers, where a council determined that the Hurons should be awarded two of the prisoners, the Algonquins the third. The Algonquins had already started to torture their prisoner and the Hurons were about to transport their prisoners home for torture by their kinsmen, who were yearning to get their hands on an Iroquois, when news of the capture reached Governor Charles Hault de Montmagny at Quebec. Montmagny had arrived in New France with the fleet that had brought Isaac in 1636 and now had a long and fruitless record of trying to establish peace among the tribes. He rushed orders to Three Rivers that nothing more was to be done with the three prisoners until he could get there.

Two days later, Montmagny addressed the Hurons and Algonquins. "Don't you see what you're doing?" he asked pleadingly. "If you kill these three men, you will only be inciting the Iroquois to seek out more of your own people to kill them. And this will go on and on until there are none of you left."

An Algonquin chief stood. "What would you have us do?"

"Release them."

Groans of incredulity came from the Indians. "If we do that," said a Huron, "they will be back tomorrow after our scalps."

"How can you be sure?"

"We know these people."

"Then," said Montmagny, "try this. Send word to the Iroquois that you will release these prisoners in exchange for three of your people whom they hold."

A Huron said: "That is not our way with prisoners."

Montmagny knew this and had been frustrated by it for years. "Don't the lives of three of your brothers mean more to you than the lives of these prisoners?" he asked, trying to reason with them. "Wouldn't you rather see your brothers home safe than merely try to avenge their deaths by killing the three Iroquois? Does a dead Iroquois erase the loss of a dead Huron or a dead Algonquin?"

The Indians muttered among themselves, then an Algonquin asked: "How do you know the Iroquois will accept an exchange of prisoners?"

"You must ask them."

"And if they refuse?"

Montmagny surveyed the council, then said: "Some of you here are Christians, made so by the Blackrobes who have worked so hard and suffered for you. You learned from the Blackrobes that killing is wrong. You have confessed to the Blackrobes your part in killings in the past, and you were forgiven. You promised to amend your lives. How do you think God will feel if you kill again for no reason but revenge? What do you think your past confessions will be worth? You must give these prisoners their freedom. It is your Christian duty. It is the only way you will ever bring about peace."

The Christian Indians stirred uncomfortably. The chiefs indicated that they wanted to discuss the matter privately, each tribe separately, and they went to different corners of the compound. When they returned, an Algonquin chief spoke first.

"We have talked this over," he said, "and we are willing to do what you say. We want peace, not only with the Iroquois but with our consciences. So we will set our prisoner free, but only if the Iroquois free one of our braves in his place."

A Huron spokesman said: "We are warriors, and we believe that when we kill the enemy who attacks us we do no wrong. But we feel now there is something in what you say about killing prisoners. Our chiefs sent us out to capture Iroquois; we have two prisoners, and we cannot release them without the permission of our chiefs. We must take the prisoners back to our villages, but we promise you we will do all in our power to convince our chiefs as you have convinced us."

Without question, an important forward step had been taken in the effort for peace among Indian tribes. The mere willingness of the delegations at Three Rivers to consider a prisoner exchange was a hopeful sign, regardless of the provisos they attached to it. A year ago, there would have been no such consideration at all. Here, clearly, was one result of the Christian influence: consciences had been sensitized and appeals could be made to them.

This condition, however, had not occurred among the Iroquois, and no one at Three Rivers or Quebec could guess how they would react to the idea of exchanging prisoners instead of murdering them. Days of anxious waiting passed —and then the news came. The Algonquins had been able to make a peaceful contact with the Iroquois—the Mohawks, in this case—and to effect an exchange. Then came word that the Huron delegation had persuaded its chiefs to approve a similar exchange, which was arranged with the Oneidas. A month later, small bands of Algonquins and

Mohawk hunters encountered each other in the woods; there was a fight, the Algonquins lost and surrendered the pelts they had collected, then there was an immediate exchange of prisoners. This was encouraging news for the French, for they hoped that the Indians, having gone this far, would soon recognize the futility in their endless skirmishes and put an end to them. The French knew that the Hurons and Algonquins, having suffered so much, were ready to discuss peace with the Iroquois, but nobody knew how the Iroquois felt, particularly the Mohawks, the leading tribe of the powerful nation.

Evidence appeared in July, when a Mohawk canoe came boldly up the St. Lawrence and swung ashore at Three Rivers. Six braves paddled the canoe, and in it were two important passengers. One was Kiotseaeton, the leading negotiator of Tionontoguen; the other was Guillaume Couture, and they announced they had come to see the Governor to discuss a peace treaty with the French. A courier raced to Quebec with the news. Overjoyed but still cautious, Montmagny instructed the courier to hurry to Montreal and ask Isaac Jogues to join him at Three Rivers. Jogues was to arrive at Three Rivers by night and not to let himself be seen either by Kiotseaeton or by Couture. Montmagny then arranged his own arrival to coincide with Isaac's, and the two men had a private conference before the peace talks were to begin.

Father Jogues wondered why Montmagny insisted on making a secret of his presence. The Governor explained: "Because of Couture. He will undoubtedly be the translator for the Mohawks. None of us except you knows the Mohawk language, and I want to be sure he translates everything correctly."

Isaac was dismayed. "Guillaume Couture can be trusted, Excellency. I have complete faith in him."

"I'm sure," said the Governor, nodding, "but we will lose

nothing by playing safe. He has been with the Mohawks two years. Two years can change a man in ways which even he does not suspect. I shall arrange a place for you to sit where you can listen without being seen. You can tell me later how Couture performs his duties."

When the council began next morning, the priest was hidden behind a partition. He listened as Couture translated Kiotseaeton's elaborate greeting and presentation of gifts, listened equally as closely as Couture translated into Mohawk the greetings and presentation of gifts for the Governor. Couture was being accurate, minutely so. Isaac wished he could show himself and take his companion-in-pain into his arms.

Then, speaking for Kiotseaeton, Couture was saying: "We have always wanted to be friends with the French, but because of your alliance with the Hurons and the Algonquins you would not give us your ear. You supported our enemies against us. You turned your back on our love. We have tried to show you our feelings by our treatment of the Frenchmen who came among us. This one who speaks for me is a son and brother of all the Mohawks. He is free to leave us whenever he wishes, but he wishes to stay with us."

Jogues frowned at this: it could not be true. If Couture could escape he certainly would.

Couture continued translating: "And the Blackrobes who came to us, we received them as friends. The one called Ondessonk we loved very much. One of our women took him as a nephew. We told him many times we would bring him back to Three Rivers the moment he asked; we told this to the Sokokis when you sent them to us, and we told it to the Dutch. But what did Ondessonk do? He ran away. We have no idea what happened to him. If he died in the forests, it is not our fault."

Isaac remembered how close he had come to being killed

[183]

at Rensselaerswyck. But what troubled him was why Couture did not take the opportunity at this point to inject the truth into his translation. He could have done it easily, without Kiotseaeton's knowledge. Was he being scrupulous? Or was Montmagny right about him? Couture went on:

"And the second Blackrobe, we found him sick and we made him well. We assured him that he had only to say the word and we would bring him back here. Instead, he begged us to release him to the Dutch, and we did so. We hoped that you would hear about these things and accept them as signs that we wanted to be friends. But you did nothing."

In his turn, the Governor pointed out that it was because of the French that the Iroquois prisoners were being released. Kiotseaeton said he had just learned this, that he was grateful for it, that he accepted the releases as the signs of friendship he had so long awaited and that he now came to find out if a peace treaty was possible. It was, Montmagny assured, depending on the terms. The terms were simple, the Mohawk said. First, a nonaggression pact between the French and the Iroquois; second, a trade agreement; third, no French intervention in the event of future Iroquois disputes with the Hurons and Algonquins.

Montmagny rejected the third term, and he asked: "Do you speak for all the Iroquois nations?" Kiotseaeton did not: the Oneidas did not think peace was possible with the French and wanted no part of the discussions, but perhaps appropriate French generosity would placate them. Nor, it was revealed, did Kiotseaeton speak for all the Mohawks: some Mohawks were still angry over the surprise attack perpetrated at Fort Richelieu when they had, he said, come to negotiate Ondessonk's release.

Governor Montmagny was not too distressed by the stalemate confronting him. Peace talks required time, wherever they took place. He said: "Tell your people that the

French want peace with all of them and that the first step toward peace must be that we forget the past. This means you must also forget your past wars with the Hurons and Algonquins. Let us hold council on this matter again, at a time when you can speak for all your brothers."

Couture, having repeated this to the Mohawks, then spoke for the chief: "Kiotseaeton says the necessary pow-wows will require many months. He won't be able to return here until the next fishing season. That would be next July."

"Tell him that is all right," said Montmagny. "Tell him, too, that we are going to put his sincerity to a test. We want to send a supply flotilla out to Sainte Marie. If it is allowed to pass unmolested, we will know he is of good heart and he will find a better heart awaiting him when he returns there next year."

The Mohawks left, taking Couture with them. Jogues was able to assure Montmagny that Couture had translated perfectly all that was said; then he revealed his uneasiness over Couture's failure to disclose in French anything he might know of the Mohawk machinations which could give Montmagny a clue of what to expect. The Governor suggested that perhaps Couture's scrupulous accuracy was indicative of Mohawk sincerity, and they had to let it go at that. The supply flotilla was delayed for three weeks, to give Kiotseaeton time to recall the roving Iroquois war bands. When it finally left, Isaac accompanied it as far as Montreal, and after weeks passed without any bad news the French assumed the trip had been a safe one, which was taken as a good sign.

But that winter there was fighting again, with heavy losses on all sides. After each fight, prisoners were exchanged, a man for a man, thereby diminishing losses somewhat, although this too was a good gesture Isaac could not help but wonder if it was also a wasted one.

July came. Father Jogues was summoned to Three Rivers for the second session of peace talks, but this time he was not required to hide himself. The Mohawk delegation was much larger—showing, Kiotseaeton said, growing evidence of the desire for peace among the Iroquois. But Isaac observed that there were no representatives from the other four Iroquois nations and no representatives from Ossernenon. He sought out Guillaume Couture; the two men greeted each other warmly.

Isaac said: "You don't seem surprised to see me."

"I knew you were back," said Couture. "Some Mohawk braves reported seeing you at Montreal during the winter."

"I didn't see them."

Couture smiled and shrugged. "You know the Mohawks."

"Yes, and so do you, Guillaume," Jogues said quickly. "Tell me, are they sincere in these peace efforts?"

"Yes, Father, I believe they are."

Isaac frowned. "They're so deceptive. What has changed them, Guillaume?"

"I think the initiative by the French in exchanging prisoners made a deep impression," Couture said. "They know it was Governor Montmagny's doing; they have a great respect for him."

"Enough to make peace with the Hurons and Algonquins as well?"

"I believe so."

"It is miraculous!" Isaac exclaimed. "And you have no doubts, Guillaume?"

"I have no grounds for doubts."

"Did you attend the council at Tionontoguen?"

"No."

"Then you have no knowledge whether they might have any secret plans?"

"No."

Isaac sighed heavily. "I wish I could escape this uneasiness." Then: "Guillaume, are you really staying with the Mohawks of your own free will?"

"You know I'm not, Father. They've promised me freedom if the negotiations go well."

"I hope they keep the promise."

"So do I."

The second session of the peace talks ended with little specific progress. The gifts were more lavish than before, and this time there were gifts from the other four nations, and the speeches were more elaborate; but Kiotseaeton reported that although the Senecas and Cayugas and Onondagas were more amenable to the idea of a treaty than they had been, the Oneidas were still against it. Could there be, he asked, a separate treaty with the Mohawks as a start? Seeing this, the others, even the Oneidas, might be more willing to come along. Montmagny did not think so: for the treaty to be effective, all five tribes must be bound by it.

A third session was set for September, and after its opening amenities Kiotseaeton requested a private meeting with Montmagny, with only Couture to be present. The subject of the meeting was not disclosed, but apparently some concessions had been made: Kiotseaeton came out with an air of victory. The French would soon be seeing further proof of the Iroquois good will, he promised, and they would be seeing him again, in January, for the final discussions and the appointment of ambassadors. Kiotseaeton offered a bonus: come January, Couture would have served his purpose and could return to the French, if he wished. The secret meeting must have gone well, indeed.

The further proof of Iroquois good will appeared shortly after the Mohawks departed: a Huron flotilla from Sainte Marie, the first in four years, came safely down the river. Father Lalemant was with it, and he explained why the Hurons had decided to attempt the journey.

[187]

"We heard about the peace talks," Lalemant said. "Lately we've had so little trouble with the Iroquois that we thought perhaps the treaty had been signed. We had to try the trip; we were desperate. We saw many Iroquois along the way, but they let us pass. Is it all over? Is there really peace?"

"There is good promise of it," Montmagny said. "Your safe journey is the best news yet."

There was other news. The summer ships from France brought the announcement that Father Lalemant had been appointed Superior of all the missions in Canada, succeeding Vimont. Jogues, as soon as he could, took Lalemant aside and told him of the forthcoming exchange of ambassadors with the Iroquois.

Isaac said: "You will certainly be consulted when the choice is made."

"I imagine so."

Jogues said pointedly: "I'm the only Frenchman here who speaks the Iroquois language."

"And you want me to recommend you?"

"Yes."

"You would rather go to the Iroquois than to the Hurons?"

"Yes," Jogues said firmly. "I pray for it."

Many years before, during his early seminary days, Isaac Jogues felt himself drawn to Ethiopia, and he prayed that he would be sent there to convert the people and that, in the course of doing so, God would give him the strength and the privilege to make the supreme sacrifice for souls. Later, during his seminary years, after the Jesuit missions in New France had been established and the indications were that he would be sent to the Hurons, Jogues frequently uttered the same prayer for martyrdom. Now he had been among the Mohawks, and he knew their ways; he knew, too, that these ways would remain unchanged until the

Mohawks were brought within the embrace of Christianity. Toward this end he dedicated his life; toward this end he uttered the same twofold prayer. This time, it would be answered.

4

At dawn on Wednesday, May 16, 1646, two Mohawk canoes waited on the beach of Three Rivers. At each stood two braves, broad-shouldered, barrel-chested, thick-waisted, and impatient. The joy of at last being on his way to the Mohawks had kept Father Jogues longer at his thanksgiving after Mass than he had realized; now he came hurrying down the hill from the Jesuit long house. With him were Jean Bourdon, a French map maker, and two Christian Algonquin braves, the latter en route to become their tribe's first ambassadors to the Iroquois. Two Hurons, both Christians, had been scheduled for the journey, but their leaders withdrew them at the last moment on the grounds that others had been chosen to replace them and would be sent to Iroquois villages subsequently. The French, however, interpreted this as an excuse to delay Huron participation in the peace pact until the Iroquois had produced further evidence of their sincerity.

Isaac Jogues was dressed in French lay clothes for two reasons. First, since he was to be the French ambassador to the Iroquois, it was decided that he should wear the clothes which the Iroquois were accustomed to seeing on the lay leaders of the colony, thereby identifying himself more with them. Secondly, the Jesuit soutane was still regarded by many pagans as the garb of the white men who had angered the spirits and thus brought on disease and famine. Jesuit leaders at Three Rivers conceded that it might be unwise for Jogues, in his role as a friendly ambassador, to arrive in the clothes of a despised Blackrobe. However, in a black box which Isaac carried was his soutane, plus the vestments and vessels for the celebration of Mass, for although he was now an ambassador of France he considered himself primarily an ambassador of God, and he was determined to say his daily Mass as often as he could. Since he intended to return to the Mohawks and stay with them he decided he might as well take along the articles for Mass and store them in Aunt's cabin until a better day.

A crowd came down to the beach for farewells and blessings. Isaac and Bourdon got into one canoe, the two Algonquins into the other. There were calls and waves of goodby and good trip. They were on their way.

For Isaac Jogues, the journey back to Iroquois territory was virtually a Way of the Cross. The party spent a night on the plateau of Fort Richelieu, where Isaac had been severely beaten his first night as a Mohawk prisoner, and each night brought him to the scene of a similar painful memory. They entered Lake Champlain: there ahead was the island where he had run the first of many gauntlets. On this night he slept there in peace.

They went on, Bourdon sketching the terrain as they advanced, producing the first maps of the area. Instead of heading southwest from the foot of Lake Champlain, as Isaac had been taken as a prisoner, they decided to portage directly to the south, in order to reach the Hudson River. They could thus go on to Rensselaerswyck, where Jogues wanted to pay his respects to the Dutch who had helped him escape. During the portage, they came to a lake which Isaac had not seen before and which Bourdon said was not on any known maps. Jogues named it the Lake of the Blessed Sacrament; years later the English named it Lake George.

Mohawk fishing parties were scattered across the lake, and in one of them Isaac found Theresa. They were able to have some privacy; Theresa went to confession, and they had a long talk. Theresa had been taken in marriage by a Tionontoguen brave and was unhappy because of it. She wanted to go home.

"I will ask them to release you when I get to your village," Father Jogues promised.

"It won't do any good," said Theresa.

"They let Couture go," Isaac said. "He is living in Quebec now."

"Maybe it is because he is a man."

"I will ask, anyway. They may grant it in order to show their good faith in the peace. Have you heard much talk about the peace?"

Theresa nodded. "Many people are happy about it, but there are others who still want war."

"What do you think will happen?"

"It depends on Kiotseaeton," said Theresa. "He is proud that he has made the peace and he is now a very important man. Some of the chiefs are jealous of him, especially at Ossernenon. If he can hold his place, there may be peace. But even Kiotseaeton says there will still be some fighting. I do not understand the whole thing."

"Neither do I," Isaac confessed. "I will see you in Tionontoguen, my dear, and try to get your freedom."

The ambassadors traveled on, reaching Rensselaerswyck on June 4. The Dominie was away with Van Corlaer at New Amsterdam; Isaac left a message that he would try to see them on a later visit. The party swung north again, to the Mohawk River, and made its way to Ossernenon.

The sight of the village on its steep hill both thrilled and distressed Isaac Jogues. He had been away from the place just three years, and yet it seemed a strange, lost place that he had seen only vaguely in a bad dream. It looked smaller than he remembered it, and dirtier. And it was quiet. Isaac knew perfectly well that the approach of his party had been observed, but no one came out to greet him.

His thought went to René Goupil and the greeting they had received. He spoke of Goupil to Jean Bourdon. There had been a giant in the little body of the holy man, and what was left of the body lay hidden in the ravine beyond the village. Isaac would go there now to pray; later he would rebury Goupil properly, putting a cross upon the grave.

They went ashore, climbed the hill and entered the village. Because it was the fishing season, many of the villagers were away, and those who remained regarded Jogues sullenly. Their lack of surprise convinced him that, like Couture, they had all learned that he had survived and had returned.

Isaac went to Aunt's cabin and was overjoyed to see her squatting at the fire. He would have thrown his arms about her, but this display of affection would have startled a Mohawk. He said: "Hello, Aunt."

"Hello, Nephew," she said. "You've come back."

"Yes. Are you glad to see me?"

"The days will tell."

"They will be good days, Aunt."

She looked away.

He asked: "May we sleep here tonight, Aunt? We go on to Tionontoguen tomorrow for a council with the sachems." Wordlessly, it was all right with her. With a glance, she ordered a boy to fetch more corn for the pot. Jogues brought in his box of Mass equipment and put it on the shelf. Aunt gave it a glance, then dismissed it, but other Mohawks in the cabin frowned at the box. To them, a box was something to be feared: it could contain evil spirits or strange animals or mysterious powers. They wondered what was in this box which Ondessonk had brought, and they were certain that it was something fatal.

The night passed quietly. Next morning, Jogues, Bourdon, and the two Algonquins walked the distance to Tionontoguen, some Mohawks accompanying them to help carry the gifts. Here the reception was different. Chiefs and sachems from all five Iroquois nations had gathered to welcome Isaac and to inform him that they all had agreed on the terms of the peace treaty. The council began with its usual ritual: the smoking of the pipe, a big meal, the exchange of gifts, interminable speeches pleading love. When Isaac spoke, he mentioned encountering Theresa and that the girl said she wanted to go home: he was confident, he said, that the Mohawks would permit this, now that everybody was friendly and there would be no more prisoners, no slaves. Kiotseaeton replied that Theresa belonged to a Mohawk brave and she ought to stay with him, but if it was true that she was unhappy and wanted to go home it would be permitted. As for slaves, Kiotseaeton added, Ondessonk himself should know better than anyone that the Mohawks never held slaves. To be sure, Jogues knew better than anyone, but he did not comment. Beholding himself, standing here, bargaining with Iroquois leaders, was a remarkable experience for Isaac. He remembered the days when they would have kicked him had he dared to open his mouth.

Then one by one the chiefs and sachems arose to acknowledge their acceptance of the peace treaty, and Jogues noted that each man made reference to "our friends, the French and the Christians." This puzzled him, but because he had already made his speech he could not speak again to ask for a clarification of the unusual delineation. When the counciil was over and the chiefs and sachems made ready to go home, Isaac approached an Ossernenon chief who was, he knew, a good friend of Aunt's and he asked: "Why did you all say 'our friends, the French and Christians'?"

[193]

The chief said: "Because you are our friends, the French and the Christians, and we are at peace with you."

"Why do you specify the Christians?"

"Because we are at peace with the Christians."

"But you are at peace with all the Hurons and the Algonquins." It was a question.

"True," grunted the chief. "With some of them."

"Which ones?"

The chief appraised Jogues dubiously. "It is the way Kiotseaeton arranged it. We will not fight the Christian Hurons and Algonquins, but the others——"

Jogues insisted: "The Iroquois are at peace with all the Hurons and Algonquins. It is in the treaty to which Kiotseaeton put his mark."

"This was a separate thing," the chief said, "which Kiotseaeton arranged privately with your leader."

Now Isaac Jogues knew. So that had been the topic of the secret session Montmagny had with Kiotseaeton and Couture. This had been the concession the Governor had made that had so obviously placated the Mohawk negotiator. In battle, how could an Iroquois tell a Christian Huron from a pagan? In the tortures and the killings, why need an Iroquois believe a prisoner's protest that he was Christian?

It was clear to the priest that he must return to Quebec immediately. That same day, at Ossernenon, he learned that Seneca and Oneida warriors were already heading north into the Huron country, feeling free to fight under the terms of the treaty. He paused at Ossernenon only long enough to resolve a problem which had arisen during his brief absence. The villagers were distressed over the black box. To calm them, Jogues repeatedly opened and closed the box, each time emptying it to show the vestments, the linens, the chalice and paten, the cruets, the missal and candles, and he explained: "When I come back, I will use these things in my worship, and many blessings will come to you and your village as a result." But the Mohawks did not believe him. After he departed, leaving the box with Aunt, they went into her long house and stood around the box, studying it, and worrying.

At Quebec, Governor Montmagny defended the secret agreement he had made during the peace talks. "Chief Kiotseaeton insisted upon that concession," he said. "He said it was the only way he could get the other tribes to agree to a peace treaty."

"But there is no peace treaty," Father Jogues pointed out. "The Iroquois are already on the warpath." He turned to Couture. "Guillaume, after two years with the Mohawks, have you not come to know them well enough to see through this scheme?"

"It was not my place to intrude upon the negotiations," Couture said defensively. "Futhermore, I believed Chief Kiotseaeton had enough power to control his people, at least the Mohawks, and that there would be no fighting."

"It is all deception," Isaac said sadly. "If the Hurons and the Algonquins ever find out about this, everything we have built among them over the past twenty years will be destroyed. We have been so careful to treat all of them equally, Christians or pagans, and now it will look as though we are throwing the pagans to the enemy."

The Governor offered: "Isn't it possible, Father, that the concession will lead to even more converts?"

Jogues shook his head. "What kind of Christians would such converts be? The Church expects its members to be willing to die for their religion, not use the Faith as a means of staying alive. You are suggesting that we bribe the Indians into the Church."

The damage was done, and the worst of the damage, Isaac felt, was that now he could not return to Ossernenon.

[195]

Knowing the secret, his return would indicate that he approved of it, however tacitly, and, knowing Indians, he realized it was only a matter of time until the concession was no longer a secret. The pagan Hurons and Algonquins would surely be infuriated; the Christians, so new in their faith, might now regard it only as a measure of self-preservation in this world, and Father wondered if he would ever again be able to baptize an Indian in good conscience, confident that the man truly believed and was not merely using the religion to save his neck.

He went back to Montreal. August passed, and in September sixty leading Huron chiefs came down the Ottawa River on their way for a council with Governor Montmagny. Angered by the repeated Iroquois violations of the peace treaty, they planned to discuss them with the Governor before resorting to retaliations. A week later, Isaac was called to Three Rivers for a meeting with Montmagny and Father Lalemant, at which the Governor told him: "The Hurons have decided to send their ambassadors to the Iroquois now, provided that you accompany them."

Jogues asked: "How were they persuaded to do this?"

"They hope that by this gesture of good faith they can convince the Iroquois to honor the treaty."

"Which treaty?"

Father Lalemant said: "Isaac, the Governor realizes now that he made a mistake in acceding to Kiotseaeton's compromise, but there is nothing we can do about it now. At least we have taken a step toward peace; with God's help, we may be able to take another—and another."

Montmagny said: "The Iroquois have already accepted you as the French ambassador. I believe they respect you now, if only for having the courage to return to them after the way they treated you in the past. Take more gifts with you, Father, and perhaps you will be able to influence them to renegotiate the treaty."

"Oh, no," Isaac said firmly. "I shall not go back as the French ambassador. I shall go back as a priest. I shall wear my soutane and say Mass, I shall baptize people when I can, and I shall try to teach all of the Iroquois to love God. I am a missionary, Excellency, and that is all I am going to be from now on." His stern tone and mien put an end to the discussion.

During preparations for the journey, Father Lalemant suggested that Jogues take along another Frenchman as a companion and assistant, and he recommended Jean de La Lande, a youngster still in his teens who, the year before, had made his way to Canada and offered himself to the Jesuits as a volunteer lay worker. Bright, pleasant, energetic, pious, he had quickly won the respect and admiration of the missionaries. Lalemant had already asked the young man if he would like to accompany Jogues to Ossernenon; Jean was eager to go.

They left on Monday, September 24. In the first canoe were Jogues, Jean and Otrihouré, the Huron ambassador; the second canoe bore Otrihouré's two adjutants; in a third canoe were several Hurons on their way home. Wednesday night, they camped at Fort Richelieu, unused for over two years, and now decaying. They talked long in the light of the fire. The two adjutants were wary of what might be waiting them in the Iroquois country; the homeward-bound Hurons said that nothing could induce them to enter the land of the Iroquois. It was Otrihouré who argued that they were all wrong, that the only Huron course of action was to confront the Iroquois at their own councils and determine once and for all the extent of the Iroquois sincerity. He argued in vain. In the morning, the two adjutants announced that they were going home. They packed the bundles of gifts in Otrihouré's canoe, wished

[197]

him luck and hurried west. An hour later, Isaac and Jean and Otrihouré were gliding down the river of the Iroquois. None of them would pass this way again.

5

Because of the many packages they had to tote across the frequent portages, they traveled slowly. Twenty days passed before they reached the place which Isaac knew was just a few hours from Ossernenon, his home. Home from now on; he would spend the rest of his life there on a quest for souls. Ossernenon would now become a mission station, and as was the custom, it would be given a Christian name. Jogues and Lalemant had decided that Ossernenon would in future reports be called the Mission of the Holy Trinity.

The prospect of returning as a missionary to the Mohawk village where he had once been a slave inspired Father Jogues to increase his pace; and when, out of the corner of his eye, he noticed a furtive movement in the trees, off to the right, he dismissed it as the flight of some frightened animal. But then, an instant later, he was certain that he had caught sight of a man, a Mohawk brave, disappearing behind a thicket. Off to the left, he heard a twig snap. Looking around, Jogues discovered that in his impatience to reach Ossernenon he had moved far ahead of his two companions; he stopped and waited for them to come into view. He was convinced now that there were Mohawks nearby, watching him, moving in on him, but he was not disturbed. A short time previous, the Mohawks had accepted him as the French ambassador and granted him freedom of travel; surely they still regarded him as the ambassador and would not harm him. Jean La Lande, however, was a newcomer

[198]

in the Mohawk territory, and Otrihouré was a Huron; both would need the priest's protection.

When the two of them reached Jogues, Otrihouré said: "I have seen some Mohawks."

"I have seen them, too," Isaac said, "but don't be afraid. I will talk to them, we will be safe." Turning, he addressed the hidden braves, calling: "It is all right, my brothers. I am Ondessonk. I have come back. These two are my friends; the Huron is an ambassador to your nation."

There was a brief silence, then a war whoop split the air, as out of the forest came a rush of Mohawks, twenty, thirty of them, their faces and bodies vivid with war paint. They raced down on the three travelers, howling, yipping, barking, encircling, dancing, waving their tomahawks. Jean La Lande watched in terror.

Father Jogues tried to calm the Mohawks, telling them: "Thank you, my brothers, thank you for the welcome, but let us go on to the village."

The fury turned to wild laughter. On signal, the braves moved in, wrenching the packages away, throwing the three men to the ground, pouncing on them, ripping off their clothes, beating them, pounding them. Jean screamed as five snarling Mohawks gnawed at his writhing body. Then all three were pulled to their feet. A few Mohawks ran ahead to spread the news, while others beat the prisoners with whips and branches, herding them toward the village at a fast pace. Isaac tried to move near Jean but the warriors would not let him.

"Pray, Jean, pray," Jogues called. "Think of God. Think of Jesus on the Cross." The boy could not speak. Tears flooded from him as the whips and branches slashed against him.

At last they came to the river, and as Jogues looked across the river, to the steep hill and the village, he saw them as he had first seen them—alive with running, shrieking, howling savages. He had no idea why the Mohawks had turned against him again. For himself, he cared nothing, and he knew that Otrihouré would be able to endure the torture that waited on the far side of the river, but the boy, Jean— Jogues would willingly have run the gauntlet twice in order to spare him.

The braves forced them to enter the water. Jogues observed that the river was surprisingly shallow; the men were able to walk across, their heads above the surface, and only Jean had to swim a short distance. Nearing shore, Isaac saw that the villagers, perhaps surprised by the unexpected arrival of prisoners, did not form the lines of a gauntlet; instead, they mobbed the riverbank and crowded the hillside, shouting and wielding their weapons.

Isaac took Jeans' hand, then said to Otrihouré: "Whatever happens, try to stay near me."

The mob was ready, many of the Mohawks knee-deep in the river. Down came the torrent of clubs and whips and iron rods and fists and feet and teeth and rocks. Grasping Jean's hand firmly, Jogues battled his way up the hill. The boy was limp and helpless, too weak even to scream in pain. The frantic vortex inched up the hill, the Mohawks fighting each other for a closer chance at the prisoners. Jogues caught glimpses of Otrihouré digging his thumbs into Mohawk eyes, sinking his knee into Mohawk bellies, wrapping his arm around a Mohawk neck.

They reached the hilltop. "Stay close," Isaac cried. More Mohawks came through the gate, blocking the path Jogues struggled to pursue. Jean fell. Jogues threw himself over the boy, protecting him; then crouching, he dragged Jean under him, butting Mohawks aside with his head. Ahead of him was the gate. He swept Jean up into his arms, letting the boy's swinging feet strike Mohawk faces, and he ran, ran through the gate, across the compound, the yelling Mohawks at his heels, until he reached Aunt's cabin and threw Jean inside. He paused just long enough for Otrihouré to see where to come, then ducked inside himself.

Aunt was kneeling over Jean, putting a cloth lightly to his face. Isaac knelt opposite her and brushed Jean's blood-soaked hair from his eyes, as the boy's broken body trembled with sobs.

Aunt said: "You should not have come back."

"Aunt, why? Why all this?" Jogues asked.

"The box."

Otrihouré tumbled into the cabin, settled near the fire and began to take an account of his bruises and bleedings.

The box. Isaac glanced at the shelf where he had left the box of his Mass equipment. It was gone. "Where is it, Aunt?"

"In the river."

"Why?"

"It contained evil spirits."

He moaned, frustrated and furious.

Aunt said: "This summer we had no rain and the crops failed, and the rivers and the lakes went low and many fish died. There was hunger and sickness, and the winter will be bad. People said the trouble was caused by the evil spirits in the box you brought."

"But I opened the box," Isaac said angrily, "and showed everybody what was in it."

Aunt dismissed this with a slight movement of her head. "You cannot see spirits; you see only what they do."

It was crushing to realize how little their friendship had affected her pagan ideas. "Aunt, do you believe there were evil spirits in the box?"

"You asked me what happened to it and I told you."

"Who threw it in the river?"

"I don't know. A woman came to me in the fields and said some braves had entered my house and taken the box and thrown it in the river. You should not have come back, Nephew. The people are very angry."

Jean had quieted; he lay on his left side, his head resting on an outstretched arm, his gaze blankly on the fire. Aunt fetched three blankets and gave one to Otrihouré and one to Isaac to wrap around themselves, and she placed one gently over Jean. The boy squirmed in discomfort. Aunt put the blanket next to him to use in the night when it would be cold. Then she put the pot on the fire.

Father Jogues sat near Jean and watched the boy's solemn face, still wet from tears. "Don't hate them, Jean."

"I don't, Father," Jean said softly. "If what they did to us is a sin, I hope God won't mark it against them. I don't want to be the reason of sin for them."

The saintly remark deeply touched Jogues. He looked at Otrihouré. The stoic Huron, his battered body hidden in the big blanket, studied the fire with vacant eyes. Isaac glanced at the fire, wondering if they would all end in flames like these.

After a while, the other Mohawks who lived in Aunt's long house came in, helped themselves at the pot, then stretched out on their blankets and went to sleep, ignoring the three prisoners whom they had brutally beaten only a few hours before. All night, there was a debate in the streets, and Jogues, kept awake by his pains and his concern for his two friends, listened to it. In loud, heated voices, most of the braves demanded death for the prisoners before the night was out, but a few of them, speaking calmly, trying to reason, pointed out that Jogues was now the French ambassador, that killing him would surely mean war, a war that would be badly timed because of the bad summer and the necessity now for all the braves to be free in the coming winter to hunt for meat to eat and pelts to trade. Furthermore, the calm ones said, there was a peace treaty which guaranteed that Christians would not be tortured or killed, and Ondessonk was a Christian. The heated braves rejected all this, reminding everyone that there would not have been a bad summer had Ondessonk not brought that black box of evil spirits into the village. Because of the hardships which had come out of this act—and would continue to come as long as Ondessonk remained alive—the Blackrobe had lost his immunity as the French ambassador and a Christian, he deserved to die, an ax should be sunk into his skull.

Listening to the flow of argument, Father Jogues judged that the majority were against him. He knew that the only circumstance keeping him alive this moment was the fact that he was in Aunt's house: they would not dare come in after him because of her importance in the village. He glanced across the fire at her; she was awake, watching him solemnly. Her eyes confirmed the conviction which slowly crept over him: he was going to die, they would all die.

This was the martyrdom for which he had prayed since his seminary years; he prayed now that he could accept it with piety, courage and equanimity. Lying there, he forgave the Mohawks for what he knew they were about to do to him, and he asked God to forgive them. He also asked for a quick death so that there would not be time for him, out of fear or pain or panic, to have a demeaning thought, say a demeaning word or enact a demeaning deed which might reduce holy martyrdom to mere murder. He asked, too, that Jean de La Lande and Otrihouré would be spared, at least spared excruciating deaths, and that he would be allowed to bear their sufferings for them. Finally, he asked that his death—their deaths—would not be in vain, that they would be for the glory of God and the salvation of souls, particularly the souls of the Mohawks.

The debate over the prisoners continued throughout the night, and in the morning, a contingent of chiefs and sachems left for Tionontoguen to consult with Kiotseaeton.

When they did not return by nightfall, Isaac assumed that the arguments had not been resolved—a bad sign. Undoubtedly, everything depended on Kiotseaeton. If he was still a powerful man and if he still wanted peace, the prisoners would live. However, the fact that the Ossernenon contingent had not as yet returned was an ominous indication that opinions were sharply divided and that Kiotseaeton, whatever he wanted, was not easily obtaining his way.

Aunt discouraged Isaac from leaving the cabin. However, villagers wandered in, to grunt at Jogues, to curse him, to blame him for the summer's bad luck, but at least here in Aunt's cabin they would not touch him. When Aunt began to prepare the evening meal, Isaac and Jean moved to the rear of the cabin to pray, as they had done repeatedly all day.

A Mohawk brave pushed aside the skin door and entered. "Where is Ondessonk?"

"In the back," Aunt said.

The brave called: "Ondessonk!"

Father Jogues came forward into the light of the fire. "Yes, my brother?"

"Come to my house," the brave said.

Isaac and Aunt exchanged a glance. Isaac asked: "Is there something I can do for you, my brother?"

"I want you to take the evening meal with me."

The invitation could not be refused without serious affront. Isaac looked at Aunt again; she lowered her face in disapproval, but she knew, too, that he could not refuse. Jogues said: "I am happy to, my brother."

Isaac adjusted his blanket and took a few steps toward the door. Jean arose to follow him, but Aunt said: "Tell the boy to stay here."

"Stay here, Jean," Isaac said. "I will be back in a little while." Impulsively he moved to Jean and embraced him, whispering: "Pray."

Aunt looked at a young brave at the fire and made a gesture with her head, indicating that the man should accompany Jogues. The Mohawk at the door pulled aside the skin drape and let the priest pass, Aunt's friend close behind him. The three men walked across the compound.

Isaac knew the Mohawk's long house and made for it, a few moments away. Arriving, he drew aside the skin that served as a door, and he entered. He had only an instant to look at the Mohawk standing just inside, a tomahawk held high in both hands. The hatchet came down fast and hard, splitting Isaac's skull open with a dull crunch. Jogues was dead before he fell to the ground. The Mohawk rolled him over, face down, and chopped off his head.

The wild howls that shook the house told everyone in the village what had happened. People bolted from their cabins into the street. Aunt moaned in deep pain. Otrihouré turned his face to the wall. Jean knew. He got up and ran to the door, but Otrihouré darted after him, grabbing him and holding him back.

The Mohawk who had come for Father Jogues was running through the streets, Isaac's head in his hand, holding it by an ear, and he was shouting: "I have his head, I have his head, I have his head!" People ran after him, yowling, laughing, clapping their hands, dancing. He spied the palisade and a thought struck him. Racing to the wall, he scurried up it as nimbly as a squirrel, and he propped Isaac's head on a pointed pole. Then he dropped back to the ground, sprawling on his back, staring up at the head, pointing at it, roaring with laughter and quivering with hysterical victory. The cheering crowd applauded him.

Some boys dragged Isaac's body through the streets, offering it to people to kick, to jump upon, to beat with sticks. A brave grabbed the body by the heels and swung it in circles, the people shrieking as they tried to elude the spurts of blood from the severed neck. On and on the savage

[205]

game went, until the body was pulp, black with dirt and red with its own blood, and the people tired of their barbaric sport. At last they threw the body into the river. Weary and satisfied, they returned to their long houses, and the village went quiet.

Jean de La Lande was inconsolable. When he was told what had happened, he moved abjectly to the rear of Aunt's house, pressed himself against the wall under the shelf and let his broken heart flood from his eyes. Over and over he said Father Jogues's name, praying for him. Gradually Jean became aware that the house had gone quiet; he had no idea what part of the night it was but, looking around, he saw that the Mohawks were asleep at the fading fires. Somewhere beyond the door, crumpled against a wall, perhaps, or dumped on the plateau, was, Jean believed, the body of the priest, the martyr. It must be buried with proper prayers and proper respect; Jean realized that this duty was his.

Earlier, on Aunt's orders, he had been confined to the house, but now Aunt was asleep, as were the other Mohawks and Otrihouré. Slowly, carefully, Jean got to his feet and made his way down the long house, past the fires to the door. He drew aside the pelt which served as the door and stepped out into the dark and cold night. Wondering where to search first for the priest's body, he moved softly away from the house.

In the shadows of Aunt's long house lurked two Mohawks, the one who had summoned Jogues and the one who had killed him. They watched Jean take his uncertain steps deeper into the darkness, until he was several yards away from the house. Then they flew at him, clapping a hand over his mouth, and they pinned him to the ground. A tomahawk made a small arc in the black night—then another—and broke open the back of Jean's head. The two Mohawks held the boy down as the struggle ebbed out of him, then one of them put a long knife to Jean's neck and cut off his head. The two of them ran quickly, lightly, across the compound to the wall, climbed it and placed Jean's head on a pole, next to Isaac's. They then returned to the boy's body, picked it up, carried it out through the gate and across the plateau, down the steep hill to the river, where, holding it by the hands and feet, they swung it high into the air, out over the water. It struck with a heavy crash. The Mohawks waited for any sign that others might have heard them or seen them, but there was nothing. They scurried up the hill, into the village and to their long houses without a word. In the morning, there was astonishment in the village when the people saw the boy's head propped on a pole next to the priest's; they all wondered who had done it, and Aunt wondered how the boy had been taken from her house.

At noon, the Ossernenon chiefs and sachems returned from the council at Tionontoguen, and they were still on the path below the plateau when the news of the two killings reached them. They were very angry, for a compromise had been reached with Kiotseaeton, and now it could not be fulfilled. Pressured by the leaders of other Iroquois tribes, Chief Kiotseaeton had agreed to repudiate the peace treaty with the Hurons and Algonquins, but he insisted that all efforts should be made for a separate peace with the French. In view of the concession the French had already made regarding Christians, he felt this was possible; he also considered it shrewd because of the prosperous trading that could be done with the French in the future. There was, too, the chief's personal position; he had initiated peace negotiations with the French despite the deep Iroquois hatred for them, and his success had lifted him to new prominence and influence in the nation. A break with the French now would threaten his leadership; he struggled to protect himself. After long arguments, he was able to persuade the other chiefs to test the idea of a separate peace with the French

by sending the three prisoners at Ossernenon safely back
to Three Rivers, providing them with gifts to placate the
French officials and with the guarantee that, in order to
supply the mission at Sainte Marie, future Huron trading
flotillas would be allowed to pass without Iroquois attacks.
For Chief Kiotseaeton, the compromise was a personal victory, as well as for the Mohawk chiefs who supported him.
But now it was an empty victory: two of the prisoners
were dead—the French prisoners, to make things worse. In
their consternation, the Ossernenon leaders decided their
only hope was to send the remaining prisoner—Otrihouré—
to Three Rivers to deliver the gifts and the guarantee, but
he did not live to deliver either. On the trip, the Mohawk
braves assigned to escort him agreed that a mere Huron,
especially a Huron who was not even a Christian, was not
worth all the hardships of the arduous journey, so they
killed him.

6

Father Isaac Jogues had died in October, 1646, but it was
the following summer when news of his death reached the
Jesuits along the St. Lawrence River. On the night of June
4, a Christian Huron knocked on the door of the mission
house at Montreal. Father Buteux answered.

The Huron said: "Ondessonk is dead, and the boy with
him."

Buteux gripped the door. "How do you know this?"

"I have this day escaped from the Mohawks. A band of
warriors captured me a month ago. They told me about it."

Buteux questioned the Huron far into the night, then
wrote down all he had said and asked him to take the report immediately to Quebec. At approximately the same
time, the ships from France were beginning to arrive on the

coast. One of them stopped at Acadia and picked up mail from New Amsterdam, left there by Dutch ships a few weeks earlier. In the mail were two letters for Governor Montmagny, one from Director-General Kieft, the other from Jan Labatie, aide to Van Corlaer, and they contained the details of the murders, details obtained at Ossernenon from the Mohawks.

Over the next few weeks, several more escaped prisoners reached Three Rivers with news of the murders. One of them had been at Ossernenon when Isaac Jogues and Jean de La Lande were killed, and he gave more details of the murders. Slowly the Jesuits were able to piece together the last hours of the two men.

In September, a party of Frenchmen went hunting a few miles west of Three Rivers, and the leader of the party was Jean Amyot, who as a boy had accompanied Isaac Jogues to the Huron country in 1636. One dawn, the Frenchmen were attacked by a dozen Mohawks. Being more skilled in the use of muskets than the Mohawks, the French fought off the Indians, killing eleven and capturing the twelfth, and they took him to Three Rivers. This was the first Mohawk to enter the French settlement since Isaac's death, and the Jesuits were eager to question him. The brave refused to talk at first, but as his resistance gradually subsided and he began to speak he told the priests even more than they had heard before.

Father Le Jeune observed: "He seems to know a great deal."

Nearby stood a Huron, who said: "This is the one who should know everything. This is the one who killed Ondessonk. I was there; I was a prisoner; I know this man. He is the one who did it."

The Mohawk vehemently denied the accusation, but it seemed to the Jesuits that only the man who had actually murdered Father Jogues could be as intimately informed as this man was. Rumors that the killer was in Three Rivers swept through the Algonquin community, and the Algonquins asked the Jesuits to turn the man over to them so that they could avenge the deaths of the priest and the boy in their own way.

The Jesuits would not permit this, and to prevent it they kept the Mohawk in their quarters. As the days passed, they had the occasion to question him on other matters, and they observed how much he appeared to know about the Christian religion. He explained that he had heard Ondessonk discuss religion around the fire in Aunt's house.

"And the things he said," Le Jeune asked, "did you think they were true?"

"No," said the man. "Not then."

"And now?"

"I do not know. I am not sure. Maybe it is true."

Thus the priest and the Mohawk began a series of talks about Christianity. A few days later, the Mohawk said: "What do you plan to do with me? You cannot keep me here in your cabin forever. I must leave someday, and the Algonquins will catch me and kill me."

"We will try to prevent that," Le Jeune promised, but he knew he could not guarantee it. There was considerable evidence that this was indeed the murderer of Isaac Jogues and Jean de La Lande, but not enough of it to subject him to French law. Sooner or later he would have to be released.

A fortnight had passed, when the Mohawk announced: "I want to be baptized. I do not want to die the way I am."

The decision surprised the priests. After questioning the man, the Jesuits agreed among themselves that he was sincere. Although a longer catechumenate would ordinarily have been required, the Jesuits realized that, because of the vengeful Algonquins at Three Rivers, there was little chance that the Mohawk, if free, would get away alive, and they decided that he should be baptized immediately.

Father Le Jeune explained to him: "In baptism, it is necessary for you to take a Christian name."

The brave asked: "What was the Christian name of Ondessonk?"

"Isaac. Isaac Jogues."

"Then I will take that name," said the Mohawk. "I will be called Isaac Jogues."

It was a week later, in late evening, when the Jesuits were all in the chapel at their night prayers, that several Algonquins entered their quarters and dragged away the Mohawk called Isaac Jogues and killed him. Upon discovering this, Father Le Jeune said: "God willing, there are now two Isaac Jogues in Heaven. This is the way the first Isaac Jogues would want it."

7

The peace treaty thoroughly shattered, there was no stopping the Iroquois now, and there would be no stopping them for more than a hundred years. They would stream north to destroy the Hurons and the Algonquins, absorbing the few who survived; attacking westward, they would conquer the Petuns, Neutrals, Eries and Illinois; southward, the Delawares and the Tuscarora would come under Iroquois power. By the time of the American Revolution, practically all Indian tribes east of the Mississippi would be dominated by the Iroquois federation. In the Revolution, the Iroquois sided with the British, and it was only with the defeat of the British and the creation of the new land of free men that the Iroquois power began to wane.

At the start, the Blackrobes were the prized Iroquois prey; the Jesuits were the first victims of the Iroquois onslaughts. In 1648, two years after Jogues's murder, the Iroquois were overrunning the Huron country. On July 4, they invaded the village near Sainte Marie where Father Anthony Daniel had gone to say Mass for the growing number of Huron Christians. He was vested and about to approach the altar when he heard the war whoops of the attackers as they set fire to the village palisade. He rushed outside and, realizing what was happening, hurriedly baptized his people and gave them absolution. Then he went back to the chapel, where the Iroquois found him. They felled him with their arrows and shots from their muskets; then they ripped off his vestments and left him lying on the chapel floor when they set fire to the building.

The next year, on March 16, the Iroquois attacked Sainte Marie, capturing Jean de Brébeuf and Gabriel Lalemant, younger brother of Jerome Lalemant who had built the mission fort. Both priests were forced to run the gauntlet nude. Then de Brébeuf was tied to a stake; a fire was set at his feet. As he began to pray aloud for the Iroquois, they made a rosary out of metal discs which they held over a fire until the plates were white-hot, then they placed it around his neck. In savage ridicule, they baptized him by pouring boiling water over his head. They knew how his nudity perturbed him, even at this moment, so they made him a skirt of thick branches, then put a torch to it. Finally they slit open his chest and pulled out his heart and ate it, and then they drank his blood.

Finished with him, they put Gabriel Lalemant to a stake and started a fire. He preached to them, begging them to give up their evil ways; to silence him they put hot coals in his mouth. He could still pray for them: he lifted his eyes to Heaven. So they gouged out his eyes and filled the sockets with burning embers. Then they baptized him, too, with boiling water just before they scalped him.

Hurons who were forced to watch the torture fled from the area as soon as they could, going south to the Petuns. Charles Garnier, who had been ordained with Jogues, was working in the Petun village of Etharite, and with him was Noël Chabanel, a younger priest who had arrived in the missions in 1644. From the Jesuit headquarters, now located on St. Joseph's Island in Georgian Bay, came orders that one of two priests should return to the main mission. Garnier decided that Chabanel should go. Thus Garnier was alone at Etharite on December 7, when the Iroquois warriors crashed out of the woods surrounding the village. Hurons and Petuns who were studying for their baptisms ran to Garnier, begging him to give them the Sacrament. They knelt around him; he was baptizing them when the Iroquois found him. An Iroquois brave, recognizing what Garnier was doing, rushed to him and sank a tomahawk into his skull. The priest fell to the ground. Exerting his last ounce of strength, he rose to his feet and resumed baptizing. The Iroquois struck again. Garnier fell. This time he was able to rise only to his knees, and he continued baptizing. Once more the brave swung his tomahawk; once more the priest dropped to the ground. He was on his hands and knees, and he continued baptizing. Once more the brave swung his tomahawk; once more the priest dropped to the ground. He was on his hands and knees when life left him.

The Iroquois knew that there had been two priests at Etharite, and now they searched for the second. When they could not find him, they threatened to kill all the villagers unless they revealed where he was hiding. Terrified, the Petuns disclosed that Father Chabanel had left the village the previous day, going northward with a small band of Christian Hurons who were escorting him to the island in the bay where the Blackrobes had moved. A dozen Iroquois immediately hurried north after them.

The mission career of Noël Chabanel had its special crosses. Although he had been a brilliant student and teacher in France, he simply could not master any of the Indian languages. He had not got beyond the stammering beginnings of a dialect in five years, which amused the Indians while humiliating him. Moreover, he did not like the Indians. Their immoralities disgusted him, their filth and bestiality sickened him, their hypocrisy left him painfully frustrated. Within a year of his arrival, he thought seriously of asking to be sent to France. But he knew it was wrong of him to feel this way about the Indians. He had become a missionary to save souls, to bring people nearer to God, and if the people happened to be Indians whose personal habits he could not abide, the fact remained that they had souls to which he had dedicated his life, for which he ought to be willing to give his life. Therefore, in his second year in Canada, he asked his Superior to go into a chapel with him, and, kneeling there, Chabanel took a special vow: he would never ask for a transfer away from the Indians and he would never accept one if it were offered; he would stay with the Indians, he would work for them as long as he lived, and he prayed that, in his love for God, God would in turn give him a love for these people.

The pursuing Iroquois caught sight of him from the hilltops on December 8, the day after Garnier's death. He and five Hurons were below, in the snow-covered valley, rushing north. As the Iroquois swept down on them, the Hurons saw them coming, and the chase was on. Chabanel realized there was no escape, at least for him.

He said to the Hurons: "I think I am the one they want. There's no reason why all of you should be captured just because of me. You continue hurrying north. I will turn west. God bless you."

He had appraised the danger correctly. When the Iroquois saw him turn west and run on alone, they ignored the Hurons and dashed after him. In a matter of minutes, one Iroquois was close enough to send an arrow at Chabanel, and it sank deep into his shoulder. The wound was serious but not fatal; he would have survived with proper care, but the Iroquois were not interested in his survival. Knowing that he would die slowly from the loss of blood, they left him there in the snow for the wolves to find.

8

Once again, months passed before news of the deaths and the circumstances reached the Jesuits at Three Rivers. Once again, as with Isaac Jogues and Jean de La Lande, it was necessary to piece the accounts together from reports of persons who had been nearby when the murders were committed or who had received firsthand details from others who were there. The Jesuits were convinced that all those who had died had suffered the deaths of martyrs for the Faith, despite the lack of irreproachable eyewitnesses, despite the fact that no physical remains were ever found. From the numerous reports, the Jesuits were able to assemble details of each death that were as accurate as the circumstances would allow. At the same time, the Society made a study of everything each man had ever written, seeking evidence of piety, holy purpose, devotion to God, the Church and the missions, a willingness to die in the act of bringing the Faith to the pagan Indians. All this took years—centuries, actually—and time and again all documentation was studied, then restudied, by the Jesuits and by the Church officials in Rome whose duty it was to determine that the Frenchmen who died at the hands of the Iroquois were truly martyrs. In 1925, Pope Pius XI announced at the Vatican that such proof did indeed exist, and he decreed the beatification of the eight men. Five years later, on June 20, 1930, the Pope proclaimed their canonization as saints of the Church.

At Midland, Ontario, once the land of the Hurons, the Canadian Jesuits erected a shrine honoring those of these saints who had died nearby: Saint Jean de Brébeuf, Saint Anthony Daniel, Saint Gabriel Lalemant, Saint Charles Garnier, Saint Noël Chabanel. And in New York State, near the town of Auriesville, a few miles west of Albany, on the very hill where Ossernenon once stood, the American Jesuits built a similar shrine, honoring the other three, Saint René Goupil, Saint Jean de La Lande, Saint Isaac Jogues. Each year on the feast day honoring the eight saints, young Jesuits, in whose veins flows the blood of their Iroquois forefathers, approach altars at both shrines and celebrate Masses, paying homage to the Jesuit martyrs and beseeching them, now in the presence of God, to intercede on their behalf for the grace, the blessings and the holiness which can lead all those who live in these lands to the Gates of Heaven.

It was, indeed, for this precise purpose that men like Isaac Jogues came here.

A CATALOG OF SELECTED DOVER
BOOKS IN ALL FIELDS OF INTEREST

100 BEST-LOVED POEMS, Edited by Philip Smith. "The Passionate Shepherd to His Love," "Shall I compare thee to a summer's day?" "Death, be not proud," "The Raven," "The Road Not Taken," plus works by Blake, Wordsworth, Byron, Shelley, Keats, many others. 96pp. 5³⁄₁₆ x 8¼.   0-486-28553-7

100 SMALL HOUSES OF THE THIRTIES, Brown-Blodgett Company. Exterior photographs and floor plans for 100 charming structures. Illustrations of models accompanied by descriptions of interiors, color schemes, closet space, and other amenities. 200 illustrations. 112pp. 8⅜ x 11.   0-486-44131-8

1000 TURN-OF-THE-CENTURY HOUSES: With Illustrations and Floor Plans, Herbert C. Chivers. Reproduced from a rare edition, this showcase of homes ranges from cottages and bungalows to sprawling mansions. Each house is meticulously illustrated and accompanied by complete floor plans. 256pp. 9⅜ x 12¼.

                                            0-486-45596-3

101 GREAT AMERICAN POEMS, Edited by The American Poetry & Literacy Project. Rich treasury of verse from the 19th and 20th centuries includes works by Edgar Allan Poe, Robert Frost, Walt Whitman, Langston Hughes, Emily Dickinson, T. S. Eliot, other notables. 96pp. 5³⁄₁₆ x 8¼.   0-486-40158-8

101 GREAT SAMURAI PRINTS, Utagawa Kuniyoshi. Kuniyoshi was a master of the warrior woodblock print — and these 18th-century illustrations represent the pinnacle of his craft. Full-color portraits of renowned Japanese samurais pulse with movement, passion, and remarkably fine detail. 112pp. 8⅜ x 11.   0-486-46523-3

ABC OF BALLET, Janet Grosser. Clearly worded, abundantly illustrated little guide defines basic ballet-related terms: arabesque, battement, pas de chat, relevé, sissonne, many others. Pronunciation guide included. Excellent primer. 48pp. 4³⁄₁₆ x 5¾.

                                            0-486-40871-X

ACCESSORIES OF DRESS: An Illustrated Encyclopedia, Katherine Lester and Bess Viola Oerke. Illustrations of hats, veils, wigs, cravats, shawls, shoes, gloves, and other accessories enhance an engaging commentary that reveals the humor and charm of the many-sided story of accessorized apparel. 644 figures and 59 plates. 608pp. 6⅛ x 9¼.

                                            0-486-43378-1

ADVENTURES OF HUCKLEBERRY FINN, Mark Twain. Join Huck and Jim as their boyhood adventures along the Mississippi River lead them into a world of excitement, danger, and self-discovery. Humorous narrative, lyrical descriptions of the Mississippi valley, and memorable characters. 224pp. 5³⁄₁₆ x 8¼.   0-486-28061-6

ALICE STARMORE'S BOOK OF FAIR ISLE KNITTING, Alice Starmore. A noted designer from the region of Scotland's Fair Isle explores the history and techniques of this distinctive, stranded-color knitting style and provides copious illustrated instructions for 14 original knitwear designs. 208pp. 8⅜ x 10⅞.   0-486-47218-3

CATALOG OF DOVER BOOKS

ALICE'S ADVENTURES IN WONDERLAND, Lewis Carroll. Beloved classic about a little girl lost in a topsy-turvy land and her encounters with the White Rabbit, March Hare, Mad Hatter, Cheshire Cat, and other delightfully improbable characters. 42 illustrations by Sir John Tenniel. 96pp. 5³⁄₁₆ x 8¼. 0-486-27543-4

AMERICA'S LIGHTHOUSES: An Illustrated History, Francis Ross Holland. Profusely illustrated fact-filled survey of American lighthouses since 1716. Over 200 stations — East, Gulf, and West coasts, Great Lakes, Hawaii, Alaska, Puerto Rico, the Virgin Islands, and the Mississippi and St. Lawrence Rivers. 240pp. 8 x 10¾. 0-486-25576-X

AN ENCYCLOPEDIA OF THE VIOLIN, Alberto Bachmann. Translated by Frederick H. Martens. Introduction by Eugene Ysaye. First published in 1925, this renowned reference remains unsurpassed as a source of essential information, from construction and evolution to repertoire and technique. Includes a glossary and 73 illustrations. 496pp. 6⅛ x 9¼. 0-486-46618-3

ANIMALS: 1,419 Copyright-Free Illustrations of Mammals, Birds, Fish, Insects, etc., Selected by Jim Harter. Selected for its visual impact and ease of use, this outstanding collection of wood engravings presents over 1,000 species of animals in extremely lifelike poses. Includes mammals, birds, reptiles, amphibians, fish, insects, and other invertebrates. 284pp. 9 x 12. 0-486-23766-4

THE ANNALS, Tacitus. Translated by Alfred John Church and William Jackson Brodribb. This vital chronicle of Imperial Rome, written by the era's great historian, spans A.D. 14-68 and paints incisive psychological portraits of major figures, from Tiberius to Nero. 416pp. 5³⁄₁₆ x 8¼. 0-486-45236-0

ANTIGONE, Sophocles. Filled with passionate speeches and sensitive probing of moral and philosophical issues, this powerful and often-performed Greek drama reveals the grim fate that befalls the children of Oedipus. Footnotes. 64pp. 5³⁄₁₆ x 8 ¼. 0-486-27804-2

ART DECO DECORATIVE PATTERNS IN FULL COLOR, Christian Stoll. Reprinted from a rare 1910 portfolio, 160 sensuous and exotic images depict a breathtaking array of florals, geometrics, and abstracts — all elegant in their stark simplicity. 64pp. 8⅜ x 11. 0-486-44862-2

THE ARTHUR RACKHAM TREASURY: 86 Full-Color Illustrations, Arthur Rackham. Selected and Edited by Jeff A. Menges. A stunning treasury of 86 full-page plates span the famed English artist's career, from *Rip Van Winkle* (1905) to masterworks such as *Undine, A Midsummer Night's Dream,* and *Wind in the Willows* (1939). 96pp. 8⅜ x 11. 0-486-44685-9

THE AUTHENTIC GILBERT & SULLIVAN SONGBOOK, W. S. Gilbert and A. S. Sullivan. The most comprehensive collection available, this songbook includes selections from every one of Gilbert and Sullivan's light operas. Ninety-two numbers are presented uncut and unedited, and in their original keys. 410pp. 9 x 12. 0-486-23482-7

THE AWAKENING, Kate Chopin. First published in 1899, this controversial novel of a New Orleans wife's search for love outside a stifling marriage shocked readers. Today, it remains a first-rate narrative with superb characterization. New introductory Note. 128pp. 5³⁄₁₆ x 8¼. 0-486-27786-0

BASIC DRAWING, Louis Priscilla. Beginning with perspective, this commonsense manual progresses to the figure in movement, light and shade, anatomy, drapery, composition, trees and landscape, and outdoor sketching. Black-and-white illustrations throughout. 128pp. 8⅜ x 11. 0-486-45815-6

Browse over 9,000 books at www.doverpublications.com

THE BATTLES THAT CHANGED HISTORY, Fletcher Pratt. Historian profiles 16 crucial conflicts, ancient to modern, that changed the course of Western civilization. Gripping accounts of battles led by Alexander the Great, Joan of Arc, Ulysses S. Grant, other commanders. 27 maps. 352pp. 5⅜ x 8½. 0-486-41129-X

BEETHOVEN'S LETTERS, Ludwig van Beethoven. Edited by Dr. A. C. Kalischer. Features 457 letters to fellow musicians, friends, greats, patrons, and literary men. Reveals musical thoughts, quirks of personality, insights, and daily events. Includes 15 plates. 410pp. 5⅜ x 8½. 0-486-22769-3

BERNICE BOBS HER HAIR AND OTHER STORIES, F. Scott Fitzgerald. This brilliant anthology includes 6 of Fitzgerald's most popular stories: "The Diamond as Big as the Ritz," the title tale, "The Offshore Pirate," "The Ice Palace," "The Jelly Bean," and "May Day." 176pp. 5⅜ x 8½. 0-486-47049-0

BESLER'S BOOK OF FLOWERS AND PLANTS: 73 Full-Color Plates from Hortus Eystettensis, 1613, Basilius Besler. Here is a selection of magnificent plates from the *Hortus Eystettensis*, which vividly illustrated and identified the plants, flowers, and trees that thrived in the legendary German garden at Eichstätt. 80pp. 8⅜ x 11. 0-486-46005-3

THE BOOK OF KELLS, Edited by Blanche Cirker. Painstakingly reproduced from a rare facsimile edition, this volume contains full-page decorations, portraits, illustrations, plus a sampling of textual leaves with exquisite calligraphy and ornamentation. 32 full-color illustrations. 32pp. 9⅜ x 12¼. 0-486-24345-1

THE BOOK OF THE CROSSBOW: With an Additional Section on Catapults and Other Siege Engines, Ralph Payne-Gallwey. Fascinating study traces history and use of crossbow as military and sporting weapon, from Middle Ages to modern times. Also covers related weapons: balistas, catapults, Turkish bows, more. Over 240 illustrations. 400pp. 7¼ x 10⅛. 0-486-28720-3

THE BUNGALOW BOOK: Floor Plans and Photos of 112 Houses, 1910, Henry L. Wilson. Here are 112 of the most popular and economic blueprints of the early 20th century — plus an illustration or photograph of each completed house. A wonderful time capsule that still offers a wealth of valuable insights. 160pp. 8⅜ x 11. 0-486-45104-6

THE CALL OF THE WILD, Jack London. A classic novel of adventure, drawn from London's own experiences as a Klondike adventurer, relating the story of a heroic dog caught in the brutal life of the Alaska Gold Rush. Note. 64pp. 5³⁄₁₆ x 8¼. 0-486-26472-6

CANDIDE, Voltaire. Edited by Francois-Marie Arouet. One of the world's great satires since its first publication in 1759. Witty, caustic skewering of romance, science, philosophy, religion, government — nearly all human ideals and institutions. 112pp. 5³⁄₁₆ x 8¼. 0-486-26689-3

CELEBRATED IN THEIR TIME: Photographic Portraits from the George Grantham Bain Collection, Edited by Amy Pastan. With an Introduction by Michael Carlebach. Remarkable portrait gallery features 112 rare images of Albert Einstein, Charlie Chaplin, the Wright Brothers, Henry Ford, and other luminaries from the worlds of politics, art, entertainment, and industry. 128pp. 8⅜ x 11. 0-486-46754-6

CHARIOTS FOR APOLLO: The NASA History of Manned Lunar Spacecraft to 1969, Courtney G. Brooks, James M. Grimwood, and Loyd S. Swenson, Jr. This illustrated history by a trio of experts is the definitive reference on the Apollo spacecraft and lunar modules. It traces the vehicles' design, development, and operation in space. More than 100 photographs and illustrations. 576pp. 6¾ x 9¼. 0-486-46756-2